J83

About the volume:

The Tyranny of the Discrete argues that in the work of trained historians, as well as amateurs, English local history is weakened by a pervasive antiquarianism. It examines antiquarianism much more closely than is common, and shows that far from being merely a pleasant amusement, it is educationally damaging and a waste of resources. The author examines the development of the main concepts in local history, and shows the importance of comparative and regional study, pursued through an ongoing and developing debate. He condemns the use of local history merely as a 'quarry', and suggests that local residents, societies and followers of family history can be brought together in the study of a new form of people's history – one which reflects the life experiences of the people concerned, and only then moves back into other, less familiar periods.

About the author:

John Marshall is the former Director and joint founder of the Centre for North-West Regional Studies and Reader Emeritus at the University of Lancaster, and is one of the small group of specialists in regional and local history which has taught in British universities. He is also actively associated with the promotion of leisure-time and 'amateur' local history.

The Tyranny of the Discrete

The Tyranny of the Discrete

A Discussion of the Problems of Local History in England

J.D. MARSHALL

SCOLAR PRESS

Published by
SCOLAR PRESS
Gower House
Croft Road
Aldershot
Hants GU11 3HR
England

Ashgate Publishing Company
Old Post Road
Brookfield
Vermont 05036–9704
USA

British Library Cataloguing in Publication Data

Marshall, John D.
    The Tyranny of the Discrete: A Discussion of the Problems
    of Local History in England
    1. England—History, Local.
    I. Title.
    942

    ISBN 1–85928–290–3

Library of Congress Cataloging-in-Publication Data

Marshall, J.D. (John Duncan)
    The tyranny of the discrete/J.D. Marshall.
        p.   cm.
    Includes bibliographical references and index.
    ISBN 1–85928–290–3 (cloth)
    1. England—History, Local—Historiography.   2. Historiography—
    England—Methodology.   I. Title.
    DA1.M27   1997
    942'.0072—dc20   96–33160
                                                                            CIP

ISBN 1 85928 290 3

Typeset in Sabon by Manton Typesetters, 5–7 Eastfield Road, Louth, Lincolnshire, LN11 7AJ and printed in Great Britain by....................

Printed in Great Britain by the Ipswich Book Company, Suffolk

Contents

Preface

The thoughts set out here have their origins in many experiences and stimulations. Some of them derive from an adult lifetime's contacts with students of local history, and with a variety of organizations devoted to that study. Some of the more unfashionable judgements find their source in experience of the adult education movement between the wars, when the idealism of the early twentieth-century founders was not yet dissipated. The world of local history studies has since become vastly transformed, of course, and it is now more redolent of hope and promise than in those rather tense and dreary days – even though its actual achievements are often profoundly disappointing.

I have owed a great deal to academic and society colleagues, especially some of those in the Conference of Teachers of Regional and Local History in Tertiary Education (CORAL), and in the Oral History Society and in the Centre for NW Regional Studies. If I gratefully acknowledge a number of these, then it will be clear that they are not (unless otherwise stated) responsible for a single statement in the following text; they have merely provided stimulus, and, often, forbearance and kindness. My thanks go, in no particular order, to John Walton, Elizabeth Roberts, Oliver Westall, Neil Evans, Gordon Forster, Alan Macfarlane, John Heath, Jenny Kermode, Trevor Raybould, John Lowerson, Alan Rogers, Charles Phythian-Adams, Christopher Elrington, Maurice Beresford, Tony Wrigley, Paul Hair, Colin Phillips, the late Eric Sigsworth, the late George Ewart Evans, Harold Perkin, Keith Wrightson, the late David Chambers (a profound influence), Hassell Smith, 'Raph' Samuel, the late William Hoskins (of course), Jim Johnson, Alan Everitt, Donald Read, David Dymond, Joan Thirsk, Anthony Sutcliffe, Angus Winchester, Ted Royle, John Widdowson, the late 'Bill' Chaloner, William Rollinson, Norman McCord, Michael Thompson, Winifred Stokes, Jim Leonard, Geoffrey Martin, Sidney Pollard, Asa Briggs, John Langton, Mike Savage, Jean Turnbull, John Saville, Paul Thompson, Mike Winstanley, Malcolm Wanklyn, Evelyn Lord, Peter Robinson, Joe Scott, Joan Clarke, Mike Davies-Shiel, John Jenkinson, John Findlater, Neil Stobbs, Robin Greaves and many others.

It should come as no surprise that several of those mentioned are researchers in local history societies.

J.D.M.
1996

'If liberty means anything at all it means the right to tell people what they do not want to hear.'

George Orwell (Preface to *Animal Farm*)

Introduction

'There is no such thing as local or regional history; there is only history.' Thus the dictum of a colleague at a conference of regional historians some years ago. There is enough force in this argument to ensure that the following discussion will be of interest to historians in general, and not merely to those whose concerns are purely local.

Unfortunately, the 'only history' argument entails the adoption of a degree of wilful blindness to the social significance of the thousands of devotees of the local variety of history, whose activities can be traced into every corner of England, or Britain, and whose consciously recognized and barely distinguished problems form much of the subject-matter of this book. These students represent amateur – and not necessarily amateurish – history and antiquarianism on a large scale, an interest which often takes effect beyond the reach of academic influence; and the students' actual and supposed interests are represented through a considerable congeries of organizations nationally, regionally and locally. The British Association for Local History (BALH) had only 1,835 members in May 1993,[1] and its admirable journal, the *Local Historian*, not many more readers. But if we add together the members of family history societies, county and city archaeological and antiquarian societies, local history societies and museum support groups ('friends' of such institutions), then we ascend not merely through the scores of thousands, but assuredly into the millions. When Lord Blake's colleagues in the Committee to Review Local History (1977–79) surveyed local history societies in England and Wales in those years, they were able to estimate that their combined memberships reached 132,000.[2] But this does not dispose of the matter, for family history societies, whose memberships include large numbers of persons who are actively committed, must outstrip the local history societies three or fourfold, and it is a matter of common observation that the enquiries of the family investigators in county and local record offices outnumber those of the 'straight' local historians by at least that proportion. We are now in the 500,000 area, and there is, in addition, a vast consumer public, somehow instinctively drawn to the past, that is reached by local press, local radio and regional or national television programmes. The presumed interests of this multitude are catered for by English Heritage.

Such media institutions and their presentations all provide information on some aspect of the local past, often in its relation to ostensibly larger subjects. It is significant that Hewison (1987) described the generality of this activity as an 'industry',[3] and it is interesting that this writer saw in the nation's obsession with stately homes and museums an indication of national decline. However, this is a crucial hypothesis which needs more than a provocative outline, and it calls for a major historical study. Hasty pursuit of such a subject can beg too many questions on the way: are not many of the same problems encountered in Europe? Yet, it must be recognized that there is something profoundly worrying in the reactions of what seems to be a manipulable public, one which is being historically or ahistorically 'educated' on a scale beyond the reach of any skilled and critical teaching of history. Any reader who would like to know more about the sheer many-sidedness of the Heritage movement (or Industry) should read the brilliantly provocative *Theatres of Memory, Vol. 1: Past and Present in Contemporary Culture*, by Raphael Samuel (1994), which dismisses the typical academic objection as snobbish and misplaced (see the Appendix to this volume). Optimists among historians – and there are some – tend to take refuge in the argument that interest in the past, the real subject of discussion, is in effect preparing the ground for the broader study of history, and so there is no ultimate cause for concern. The argument set out here may not please such easily mollified colleagues, and in Chapter 3 discusses the negative, anti-human and escapist effects of antiquarianism, which is thereby seen as an educational blight, one that kills curiosity as it romanticizes the past. Heritage is above all a miserable substitute for the basic historical education of the citizen (and of the nation's children), and the case is pursued further in Chapter 7.

Very properly, professional historians prefer to teach history, just as they commonly avoid acting as adjuncts to the Heritage Industry, and it must here be admitted that a heavy responsibility falls on very few.[4] University specialists in local and regional history are not numerous, and much of the post-war standard bearing in this field has fallen on two groups of colleagues: the philosophical leaders and followers anchored at the University of Leicester, whose influence is examined in some detail, and the adult education specialists who have turned group participatory local history study into a field that has promised more than it has achieved. In addition, much local history has been propagated by adult classes run by part-time tutors, some of whom have represented in themselves all the weaknesses discussed in this book. Over and beyond such considerations, the study of local and, above all, regional history has left a mark in more than 50 British universities in the last generation, while the parts played by non-history departments (like those of geography and sociology) have not been negligible. However, the combined strength of all these specialists has never exceeded more than a few hundred.[5] Yet, if those who have devoted their lives to history are to see its benefits further spread, then there is much to do by way of civic obligation. The appearance of well-supported local history diploma, certificate and MA courses in the older and newer universities gives hope and encouragement. But it is still vastly important to make contact with a broader public, a point which is heavily stressed in Chapter 7.

The potential influence of this small band of teachers has often been limited – rather than spread – by the vast and fragmenting range of subject topics that can be denominated local, urban or regional, and the general blighting effect of fragmentation, especially in local historical studies, is discussed in Chapter 2. It should be borne in mind, also, that the ultimate and distinguishing attribute of these forms of locational history is that they can be used as a medium for creating *syntheses*, rather than long and conscientious lists of subject-headings of the kind that one sometimes encounters in the Victoria Histories of the Counties of England (VCH). Yet another limiting influence on the studies of local and regional history has been that of a wider historical and academic community, which has been fond of treating such local work as *instrumental* in providing examples for wider and more portentous operations – the commonly used metaphor, 'quarry', implies a great deal – and nobody struggling to handle and direct a multitude of local historical strands wishes to be seen merely as the proprietor of a quarry. Hence, historical demographers will use localities for comparative instances and illustrations while only partly designing to illuminate, or even to understand, the fuller history and character of the localities surveyed. In this sense, instrumentality is a matter for serious discussion, and that assumption has been made throughout. Relatively few areas have a really full or satisfactory history which answers present-day questions, and very often the instrumentalizers are hardly to be blamed. Meanwhile, the problems of interpreting both urban and regional history are seen as increasingly complex, and only now is the history of small towns being adequately reviewed, just as studies of the interrelations of town and country are showing signs of transcending accounts of local migration of populations. Sadly, the old and overworked idea of 'regional' history as economic and social history using convenient county boundaries dies very hard, and it is said that even master's degree students in some centres scarcely move beyond it.

Although there can be some satisfaction that the case for regional historical study has been made, nearly all the periodical literature on the subject seems to adopt the instrumental approach, in the sense that national themes are adapted to regional raw material and sources, and very few regions are studied for their own peculiar problems,[6] or for themselves. And, of course, it goes without saying that a real understanding of parts of 'the nation' might considerably enhance understanding of the whole. Unfortunately, the comparative study of regions is still in its infancy, perhaps because nobody has as yet managed to put forward bases of comparison that are generally acceptable. Perhaps fortunately, counties, which are the possessors of archives, do in fact generate statistics and other comparables, which in turn make possible somewhat crude historical comparisons and contrasts. Even more importantly, county (and regional or sub-regional) data provide background for the study of smaller or microcosmic units. It is this background which has been lacking in local historical discourse relating to great tracts of England; in its absence, there has been a dubiously justified historical stress on the single place and the local 'community', and much of the present study is, understandably, concerned with this anomaly and the misunderstandings that have arisen from it.

It is hereabouts that the reader will begin to appreciate the import of the title of this study. We have just touched on the problem of the discrete place, examined without a visible territorial framework to give it meaning (and no amount of airy stuff about the *genius loci* will mean much unless other nearby places are examined too). However, the 'discrete' of the title relates just as forcibly to the single or the isolated fact, the document seen in isolation, the county narrative hanging in mid-air, and the inconclusive study that will probably never call out an answer or an echo in the territory over the road or over the river. It relates to the discrete fragments into which some specialized branches of historical study are in danger of breaking; and it connects with the wholly spurious (and discrete) particles of erudition which are the consequences of the misuse of documents in easily accessible search-rooms.

If this small book is addressed to anybody at all, it is to the citizen who is puzzled by a real problem relating to his or her forbears. Sadly, he or she will not easily turn to these pages unless they have travelled a longish way on their studies. So, the volume is freely recommended to students taking local history qualifications at college or university, who will indeed connect with the topics under discussion, and who will find that these are among the very few writings on approaches to local history that raise, however simply or basically, philosophical and theoretical as distinct from procedural, document-related and topic-related problems. Tutors may be provoked and even prejudiced by some of the arguments set out here, because there is nothing like a safe, comfortable, received legitimacy of ideas to set the framework for one's routines and courses – and many groan beneath burdens. On the other hand, a good many colleagues may be glad that there is at least a debate to develop.

The discussion will also satisfy the English man and woman's desire to hear both sides of a story; much of the responsibility for providing the main source of local historical wisdom has hitherto fallen on the shoulders of Leicester colleagues, who have comported themselves honourably and ably for nearly two generations, and whose 'school' has provided such theory as many teachers of local history felt that they needed. The consequent absence of debate has been an unhealthy state of affairs in a subject that is discussed in graduate seminars. A minor and artificial substitute debate has been speculatively put in motion, that which sets regionalists against localists, and that which tries to set local folk-knowledge against academic training,[7] but these gestures represent despair, and miss the point entirely.

One final comment, which is also a warning: this discussion could all too easily be represented as an 'attack' on amateur local history, or, worse, as an onslaught on the local historians themselves. On the contrary, the approach set out here refuses to treat such students as second-class citizens, fit only for the bread and circuses of the world of Heritage. It assumes that there is one set of painfully agreed standards only, by which all historians must work and regarding which all must ultimately agree. It is most certainly in harmony with the idea of giving amateurs encouragement and support, but it regards the adoption of double or separate standards as a betrayal. It is to be hoped that this statement is plain enough.

A word on terminology. 'Local' and 'regional' are widely employed but how local is local? What is 'localized'? A study of a locality can be more or less localized in its approach; it may or may not stay in narrowly defined boundaries, and it may very sensibly reach into a district, or even a region, in order to make points or comparisons. On the other hand, 'local history' has habitually been used to denote something both rural and restricted, and such heavily employed phrases need re-examination. 'Localized' can also embrace the urban. Meanwhile much general social or other history does draw evidence from localities, and the word employed here is 'locational'; however, 'localized' is used more often in the body of the text. Other key words in the discussion, such as 'instrumental', or 'instrumentalism', speak for themselves.

Notes

1. Information by courtesy of the Administrator, British Association for Local History.
2. Report of the Committee to Review Local History (Blake Committee) (1979), issued on behalf of the Standing Conference for Local History, London, 10.
3. Hewison, R. (1987), *The Heritage Industry: Britain in a Climate of Decline*, Methuen: London, *passim*.

4. Regional history was established at the University of Leeds in the 1960s, and regional centres appeared soon afterwards at the University of East Anglia (1968) and Wolverhampton Polytechnic, followed by the University of Lancaster. Meanwhile, local history was used in research or taught in a succession of civic universities during the following 20 years; for a useful survey, see Garside, P. (1978), 'Local History in Undergraduate History Courses', *Local Historian*, **13**, (8). In some departments the subject-matter took the form of urban history.

5. An accurate calculation of all members of university staffs teaching local and regional history is rendered very difficult by the fact that local history is often taught through adult groups by part-time lecturers. In 1992 the combined memberships of the Conference of Regional and Local Historians (mostly internal history staff members), and of the Association of Tutors in Local History (adult educationalists), with an additional allowance for teachers who were not members of either, totalled about 300. Also, many economics, geography and sociology departments included a local element in their teaching. Since 1992, there has been a loss of adult education staff through retirement and other causes, some having moved into internal posts.

6. Regions often have distinguishing features such as relatively high (or low) crime rates, apparent high or low literacy, relative concentrations of book clubs or libraries or grammar schools, greater or lesser losses of people by migration, high incidences of industrial disputes, numbers of trade union branches or lodges, concentrations of wealthy people, stresses on large or small farms, and so on. The present writer long ago discovered that the Cumbrian counties had high bastardy rates in the nineteenth century, and this called for explanations: see Marshall, J.D. (1995), 'Out of Wedlock; Perceptions of a Cumbrian Social Problem in the Victorian Context', *Northern History*, 30, 194–207.

7. Rogers, A. (1995), 'Participatory Research in Local History', *Journal of Regional and Local Studies*, **15**, Summer, 1–14. A most interesting contribution to the much more general debate on the nature of local history is by Skipp, V.H.T. (1981), 'Local History, a New Definition, Part 1', *Local Historian*, **14**, (6), 325–31; and *idem* (1981), 'Local History, a New Definition and its Implications, Part 2', *Local Historian*, **14**, (7), esp. 396–8. The author of these articles saw the present organization of English local history as being generally beneficial, and looked at the former much as Burke did at the British constitution. Antiquarianism, as he saw it, is not a threat. Readers will understand that the present writer might have a point in dismissing such complacency not as 'Burkian' but as Panglossian.

CHAPTER ONE

Local History in England:
The Formative Influences

English local history, viewed in any serious manner, belongs to the twentieth century. It has antiquarian roots in the soil of earlier centuries, but its blooms, varied as they are, have been nurtured by professional nurserymen – academic historians in the great mass production centres for higher education, modern universities. The plant (and its distribution throughout rural and urban England is a matter of interest) differs from almost any other species of historical study in the apparent strength of its appeal to large numbers of leisure-time and extra-mural students. Because of this appeal, local history is often seen to be of 'political' or campaigning importance to those concerned with teaching it; yet, curiously, critical discussions of its history, character and applications are exceedingly rare.[1]

Local history, like some forms of political history, has been influenced by the antiquarian activities of earlier centuries, and this antiquarianism has been the province of the leisured or comfortable amateur.[2] It has been customary to attach importance to this long tradition in local recording, and the late W.G. Hoskins, who was no admirer of the more mindless manifestations of antiquarianism, somewhat paradoxically opened his study of *Local History in England* (in the first edition of 1959, and in succeeding editions) with an enthusiastic account of the surveyors of gentry possessions and antiquities within the counties of England. Now, these massive recitations and celebrations of wealth and usually unchallenged landowning power are of considerable interest to the social historians of the periods of British history concerned; yet they are thoroughly bad models for the aspiring local or regional historian, and it is difficult to know why Hoskins and others have drawn attention to them.[3] They are, of course, of occasional use for certain kinds of reference, but they have often been supplanted by the Victoria Histories of the Counties of England (VCH), the hundreds of volumes of which are organized works of real weight and utility. It seems that propagandists for local history are altogether too anxious to seek respectability through antiquity when they advertise the older county surveys as 'history'.

Hoskins, in any case, had no illusions about the earlier county surveyors, whose compilations were recitational, repetitive and sometimes obsequious, and, late in his career at Leicester, he described their works thus:

> They varied in their emphasis and treatment, but basically they had one thing in common and that was that they continued to be written by gentlemen for gentlemen, with all the limitations of subject that that implies. They were interested mainly in one social class – the landowning class – its pedigrees, heraldry, possessions and appendages like the parson and the church; though occasionally a more imaginative writer would devote a page or two to the working conditions of the labouring class.[4]

However, he did misleadingly use the word 'histories' to describe such volumes, the point being that the study and practice of history has so developed in the nineteenth and twentieth centuries that real, and even dangerous, confusion can be caused when this descriptive term is applied to antiquarian studies. This is very far from saying that such compilations are useless for all purposes, or that 'histories' was not once used to describe them with perfectly honest intent.

Hoskins's objection to such works was that they were socially one dimensional. He could have added that county antiquarianism, expressed in a powerful tradition which these works helped to reproduce and to underpin, is still alive and well notwithstanding the fact that its journals have readily printed articles by academics (as in the case of Hoskins himself). Its largely unconscious prejudices still influence aspirant local historians throughout Britain, especially those individuals who, in pursuit of family history, evidently wish to attach themselves through genealogical discovery to the rich and titled.[5]

Antiquarianism, as will be shown in Chapter 3, is more widespread and deeply rooted than even this comment would suggest. Meanwhile, the recorders and compilers of previous centuries have provided a legacy which has been so abiding that British local history – or antiquarianism – really does seem to be imprisoned in its own past.

This legacy embraces the common administrative divisions which have dominated British local and political history since the Middle Ages, namely the parish and the county. The antiquarian recorders religiously adhered to these divisions from the sixteenth to the nineteenth centuries, while directories, gazetteers and VCH scholars reproduced them, and local government was constructed upon their use and application. It is as well to emphasize that these are political, legal and even (in the case of the county and its lieutenants) military divisions, bounded territories in which power is applied and the law is operated. Although local historians have often been unwilling to discuss the possibility, the steadily growing demands and claims, first of economic and then of social history, have cast doubt upon the reality and the uses of these divisions. If we, for example, trace the growth of a local industry, sooner or later we shall find it crossing administrative boundaries (although, following Pat Hudson's work,[6] we may find industry to be influenced by manorial control or the lack of it). If we trace social linkages and population movements alike, we shall certainly find each of these crossing mere administrative boundaries. An old boundary can have a social effect, as Charles Phythian-Adams and his Leicester colleagues have demonstrated,[7] but this is a different argument and, briefly, early modern and modern societies – including industrial societies – cannot be contained satisfactorily within old and fixed administrative boundaries. We may look for them within this or that boundary or framework, but we must not assume that the societies themselves are even approximately confined there, or halted at the boundary.

No present-day historian would contradict this proposition for a moment. Yet the simple reality is that much of English, or British, local history, including the non-antiquarian, genuinely historical kind, has been contained within the bounds of the parish, just as several of our major territorial economic histories (of which more is said below) have been set within county frameworks. Is this the consequence of the sheer weight of antiquarian tradition, or has some other type of influence been at work? Let us consider the county first of all. It is possible – and these are the most provisional of suggestions – that the county, whether an economic and social reality or not, is so much of a widely accepted *symbol* of convention in national (and regional) life that it has been regarded as necessary to write about it and to trace histories within its area. Then, one must remember that the county seems to acquire more and more weight as one goes back in time; it is clearly an important division in medieval terms and, as a major debate has indicated, it has had a degree of social significance for members of the gentry – in the seventeenth century.

How essential a social framework was the county? We may take due note of gentry power-mechanisms after the formation of county councils in 1889, but this would scarcely justify writing social history within the county framework, unless the work was done for a very specific purpose.[8] What we seem to be witnessing is the working of a mixture of conventionality and convenience, it being understood that counties have rich archives and large literatures and that they are excellent generators (or repositories) of statistics.[9] This last has proved to be a very important consideration, because the statistics relate also to parishes, and the parish is for practical purposes the base unit in county affairs, as well as the foundation-stone of the diocese. The statistical (and raw factual) framework of both territorial units, parish and county, is formalized in the VCH volumes and in the successive *Statistical Accounts* for Scotland. The decennial census, too, used both the counties and the county divisions, the parishes and the hundreds, just as the civil registration authorities of post-1838 used counties and poor law union areas, again composed of groups of parishes. There is, in fact, an enormous compulsion to make use of parish data, whether the latter are derived from parish registers, tax lists, tithe schedules, agricultural returns or the products of a score of other officially originated surveys and documents.

Notwithstanding such documentary temptations, few parish histories of any pretension were written before the middle years of the twentieth century; a few from the late Victorian or Edwardian period stand out (Cowper, 1899, much admired by Hoskins; Davies, 1909; Armitt, 1916), as imaginative offerings by leisured people. The disjointed compilation by the vicar was much more common. Three exterior factors influenced the development of twentieth-century local history, whether in its local parish (or small town) or in its county form. The first and most obvious was the growth of an element of professionalization, but this factor was very closely related to another – the development of economic-with-social history as a broad and powerful specialism. The third factor, unconnected with the first two, was a massive increase in the easy availability of records to the academic world and the leisure-time user alike; it is this factor, or its previous absence, that goes far towards an explanation of the timing of the development of local, or localized, history in Britain. Needless to say, this accession of material does not wholly explain the palpably increased general popularity of the subject after the Second World War, and it is likely that the combined effect of two world wars produced a nostalgic, patriotically inspired or sentimental view of the imagined rural community, which in turn stimulated local history.

Such bucolically charged sentiments certainly existed in Victorian and Edwardian England, and this strand in British thought was interwoven within a broader literary tradition. The interrelations of 'Englishness' (usually of the southern kind) with a form of middle-class literary ideology and with awareness of particular regional landscapes, influenced (for example) the biographical-cum-landscape writings of Edward Thomas;[10] and it is worth noticing that Thomas was active, in this case as a journeyman and hack, well before the First World War. While it is undoubtedly true that sensitivities to regional identity have been strengthened by major works of literature, whether (to list a number of the most obvious) by Burns, Crabbe, Hardy, W.H. Hudson, Cowper, Clare, Gilbert White or Wordsworth, it is both misleading and untrue to argue that local and regional history have benefited in their respective ways from any particular literary tradition. It is in any event very difficult to show that such movements or fashions have prompted phases of local historical writing, although it is certainly the case that professional writers and belleslettrists have written regional surveys and guides, often of a historically dubious kind, while, on the other hand, some very capable regional novelists have used local historical material with effect.[11] Accordingly, the indebtedness is from literature to history, and not the other way round. It remains true that a good localist historian often requires the insights of the poet, and a sensitivity to movements, moods and changes of regional culture is a very necessary part of his or her equipment. However, it is also true that where professional literary men and women venture into the field of local history, the result is likely to be a form of self-indulgent antiquarianism – the late Geoffrey Grigson's topographical and natural-historical surveys provide many relevant examples. Notwithstanding this criticism, Grigson, an outstanding poet, wrote in a frequently absorbing manner. A great deal of local history is abominably written, often in an attempt to seem scholarly, and has a decidedly unedifying tradition in this respect.

The effect of war as well as literary tradition on local history is, to return to the main argument, a worthwhile and proper subject, and this is plainly a field that calls for the attentions of the specialist surveyor. It can be seen as highly significant that Terrick Fitzhugh, the founder-editor of the *Amateur Historian*, wrote in his first editorial in Autumn 1952 that

> during the war, the threat to our way of life and our ancient cities turned particular attention to the past from which our traditions have stemmed. With the removal of the threat, the interest has not lessened; rather, with the records once more available, it has flowed into a widespread active curiosity about our history, and especially about the history of our towns and villages ... [12]

Fitzhugh's small publishing enterprise (the *Amateur Historian* later became the *Local Historian*, which remains in existence) was a response to amateur interest but, as may be noted, it had the backing of professional historians who were influenced by a number of factors – radical or revolutionary politics or, not irrelevantly, by the adult education tradition of Tawney, Temple, Green and Mansbridge, with its encouragement of independent self-education by the ordinary citizen.

Tawney and the Hammonds were also associated with a radical and even a Marxist tradition in the relatively new discipline of economic history. This was, in the immediate post-war years, growing away from the main stem of general and political history, and it was to have some profound effects on the serious writing of the local variety. There was also a developing conflict within the teaching and study of economic history, between Hammondites and anti-Hammondites, which influenced the nature of some key exchanges, and which was considerably exacerbated by the onset of the Cold War. This contest had begun to make itself felt in the 1930s,[13] but it flared up with greater vigour after 1945. There is a case for arguing that this often bitter underlying conflict, which was in essence political, led to a noticeable intellectual conformity in the adult education movement[14] and in other branches of academic life. It is extremely difficult to show what its effects were at a given time and place, but some pressures towards orthodoxy and a crippling lack of debate certainly came from that direction. (Local history could be seen as 'neutral'.)

Let it be said at once that the newly founded and small Department of English Local History at the University of Leicester (established in 1948) kept well clear of any overt association with ideologies. But, even if H.P.R. Finberg, the head of the Department in the 1950s, had not been a historian deeply conservative in temper, that unit would no doubt have been obliged to ignore any temptation to take sides. W.G. Hoskins, the founding head of the Department, was however a liberal radical with much sympathy for the local amateur student and some affinity with a critical-minded 'Hammondism'. He was not a Marxist, but exhibited a mixture of attitudes, refusing to interest himself in Cold War politics and history. When a young lecturer at Leicester in the 1930s (in 'commerce', i.e. economic history), he had been considerably influenced by Tawney, and his attitudes to local societies and wealthy élites continued to bear the marks of Tawneyite analysis. Hoskins also interested himself in local and county history for their own sakes, rather than as instruments for a wider study of economic history, becoming an expert on Leicestershire, central Midlands and some aspects of Devonshire history. He was particularly interested in agrarian change. Hoskins carried within himself some of the contradictions in the developing subject of local history, and that is why a consideration of his personality *qua* historian has much relevance to this argument.

This characterization of Hoskins is of great importance for another reason. Nearly all the pioneers of regional economic history in the 1920s and 1930s had written primarily with a view to strengthening national or economic history in general, and only secondarily about economic or industrial regions. J.D. Chambers, an individual who reflected very faithfully some of the current and subsequent attitudes among economic historians, explained the main purpose of his elegant study, *Nottinghamshire in the Eighteenth Century*, in these terms: 'it is essentially an attempt to use local history in the service of general history'.[15] This almost certainly applied to the regional industrial histories by Heaton, Daniels, and Court, especially if one substitutes 'economic' for 'general'. About other major regionalist historians of the inter-war years, there is more doubt: A.H. Dodd's great study of North Wales was the work of an all-round or generalist historian trying to discover something of the deeper realities of industrialization, while the work of A.P. Wadsworth on *The Cotton Trade and Industrial Lancashire* (1931), undertaken with Julia Mann, and G.H. Tupling's remarkable pioneering study of agrarian history and industry in Rossendale (1927), were alike the testimonies of scholars who resembled Hoskins in that they had abiding local roots and interests. Tupling became an expert on Lancashire local history,[16] just as Hoskins did on that of the central Midlands and Devon. The mark of a man or woman who is engaged in using local or regional history as an instrument, or for illustration of more general themes, is that (in most cases) he or she does not return to it, whereas a scholar who is concerned with the illumination of the region or area for its own sake will continue to publish material on it. In this connection, it may be remarked that Chambers, notwithstanding the frank comment in his *Nottinghamshire in the Eighteenth Century*, was very much a man of a region, and his extended essay, *The Vale of Trent, 1670–1800*,[17] represents an important step forward in the understanding of regional transformation examined independently of county frameworks.

Almost all of the inter-war pioneers in regional economic history had used county areas as a matter of convenience. Indeed, Chambers himself, in his *Nottinghamshire*, had shown so much incidental insularity that he made hardly any sustained references to adjoining Derbyshire, which shared a border coalfield with Nottinghamshire, or to Leicestershire, which shared a framework knitting industry with its two northerly neighbours. The author later recognized the weaknesses of this approach, but it has to be recorded that any lessons that Chambers managed to exemplify have been ignored by the generality of would-be regional historians and their publishers, and that conventional county chronicles and recitations continue to be published. (However, this is not to argue that county studies cannot be useful sometimes, especially in the hands of VCH editors; otherwise the county is a pint pot into which everything is poured.)

As Chamber's 1932 comments showed, local history was seen by him as 'antiquarian lore'[18] to be given relevance by economic or general history. But as economic history developed, it began to act as a vehicle for *locational* history of different kinds, local, urban and county or regional. A very fine pioneering example of locational economic-and-urban history was W.G. Hoskins's *Industry, Trade and People in Exeter, 1688–1800* (1936), which indicated the potentiality for economic and social analysis of a seventeenth-century town. This book was far removed from the reverently dedicated booster history, or the semi-antiquarian celebration of a town's institutions to which the Victorians had made historians accustomed. However, Hoskins was at this early stage becoming immersed in Leicestershire agrarian history, and he published a paper on 'The Fields of Wigston Magna' as early as 1937.[19] He identified himself even at this period with what may be called the archaeology of rural history – visual as well as documentary evidence for field systems, the study of deserted villages, trackways, springs and water supplies, and ancient boundaries or ditches.

During and just after the Second World War Hoskins made a special study of deserted villages in Leicestershire and the central Midlands, and this archaeological approach, developed in association with M.W. Beresford,[20] greatly conditioned Hoskins's view of the framework and subject-matter of local history. In Hoskins's case, the die was already cast by 1945, even though he was to be immensely productive in the 20 or so years that followed. His local history was investigated in the open air, was mainly rural and agrarian, and was vigorously concerned with the social life of the peasantry and of countrysides. It was conducted on a generous time-scale, for Hoskins ultimately practised what he preached when he urged the chronologically elongated study – carried out over six or seven centuries – of parish 'communities' or societies.

Both Hoskins and his colleague H.P.R. Finberg seem to have had no difficulty in agreeing that the proper concern of the local historian was 'the local community', studied over long periods in such a manner as to embrace its 'origin, growth, decline and fall'.[21] But a mass of problems and obstacles lay concealed within this simple formulation. There was, first of all, the basic matter of defining a community, and Finberg (who in 1951 succeeded Hoskins as head of the Department of English Local History) seemed to brush this problem aside as an unprofitable distraction.[22] It is true, of course, that sociologists do not agree over the meaning of 'community', but their activities imply a certain intellectual rigour,[23] and the Leicester pace-setters seem to have fallen much too easily into the assumption that a community would reveal itself fully formed in the course of documentary investigation. Moreover, nobody associated with the Leicester team succeeded in showing convincingly, during the first decade of their operation, how the movements in the fortunes of a community might be demonstrated on this grand chronological scale and, in particular, what 'decline and fall' really meant. As Finberg afterwards argued,[24] one had to have a clear perception of community as a 'closely integrated social formation' before one could write about its break-up (and by inference, decline), and the general concept of the local community, whether ultimately useful or not, did provide a strong potential springboard for debate.

Yet, the crucial debate was lacking, and the reason was not hard to see: one or two pioneers could not provide it, and there were few people inclined to take it up. The whole area of local history was, and for many years remained, thinly professionalized and staffed by persons who seemed capable of developing a contentious but rational debate. Curiously, Hoskins's work of the 1950s showed traces of the 'ecological' approach to the community promoted by the US sociologist Amos Hawley (Hawley, 1950), and it is not suggested that the Leicester scholars did not employ what seemed to them to be useful ideas from parallel disciplines. Sociologists were deeply interested in urban and rural communities during the 1950s and 1960s, and their contribution is referred to in Chapters 4 and 6. Whatever the case, the popularization of local history began to take precedence over the campaign for intellectual rigour in the field. Sympathetic historians, on the other hand, preferred to use local history as a 'quarry' or as a medium for the occasional creative, but mainly empirical, exercise. As regards the influence of the Cold War, Chambers and his friend and colleague W.E. Tate used local and regional examples to establish a new orthodoxy in the interpretation of a major theme in local history, that of the social effect of parliamentary enclosures.[25] But no real contest followed, and a generation of acceptance was ended only when a group of critical historians challenged Chambers's methodology,[26] thus creating a more balanced view of enclosures.

This stark example gives some insight into the intellectual timidity that surrounded the use of local historical evidence; yet, Chambers's standing as a regionalist carried much weight, and Cold War orthodoxies were challenged only by the very bold (and by the members of the Communist Party's Historians' Group). Hoskins, as an agrarian historian and a good Tawneyite, is known to have been critical of Chambers's approach to enclosures, but the former did not engage himself in the discussion.[27] This atmosphere was scarcely more conducive to vigorous debate and bold thinking[28] than was the rigid Soviet-type conventionality in history and philosophy.

It would be simple exaggeration to suggest that the orthodoxy which enveloped local history was of the latter kind, but the more general ambience of the time may well have encouraged it, and conformity in one sphere will spread into others. For the rest, a shortage of guiding themes, a largely inevitable absence of training based on historical concepts and wide experience, and a consequent lack of well-founded professionalization, together ensured that the main ideas put forward by the devoted Leicester local history staff were accepted almost without question by those who taught or organized the subject. However, it should also be recognized that the history-of-the-community concept put forward from Leicester fitted very well into almost any form of local history teaching, good and bad, historical or antiquarian, pretentious or otherwise, and its popularity certainly had little to do with the actual aspirations of the Leicester teachers. Instead, Hoskins and his colleagues were perhaps fortunate in that they touched upon quite a different nerve of public awareness, that relating to the discovery of the countryside, historical and archaeological, and they thereby reached a much wider public than that simply concerned with adult education or teaching. This, however, came somewhat later in the post-war decade.

Meanwhile, the chronologically elongated view of local history, if not the local-community idea, received support from an influential quarter – from R.B. Pugh, then General Editor of the Victoria Histories. Pugh's *How to Write a Parish History* (1954) ran through several editions in the 1950s, and adopted without reservation or apology the 'quarry' view of local history as enlarging the understanding of the national variety. Local history, to this authority, was essentially a technique of research, covering a wide range of sources and a large selection of topics. The topics themselves ran from Domesday through to the analysis of occupations in the mid-nineteenth-century census schedules, and they suggested clearly enough that a disjointed and uneven story could emerge if the parish was studied over a long period. At the same time, Pugh elevated the function of local history into that of supplier of detailed information across the parishes of the nation. Here, indeed, was the subject-matter for an important debate, and Finberg objected to Pugh's instrumental view of local history, asserting that 'local communities ... have a history which deserves to be studied for its own sake'. It was here that Finberg made his now well-known distinction between 'local history per se and national history localized',[29] although, unfortunately, the argument here was not developed as it should have been, and much confusion has been created by it, in that many students have interpreted it literally.

One of the late Ralph Pugh's VCH colleagues, W.R. Powell, then provided more material for a potentially developing debate by challenging the Leicester notion of the 'fall' or the 'disintegration' of a community. Hoskins had given his own variant of Finberg's concept by envisaging 'the growth, the perfection and the final disintegration of a local community in a given neighbourhood'[30] (a formulation which he continued to use in his textbook *Local History in England*), and Powell retorted that 'no human community can be said to have disintegrated while it includes people who are born, go to school, work, play, make love and die'.[31] Finberg, for his part, riposted that 'it is obvious that Mr. Powell is not really envisaging anything like the closely integrated social formation which has been an ever-present, not to say obsessive, reality for many thousands of people through the centuries'.[32] But Powell had also pointed out that many parish 'communities' could not be adequately studied owing to a relative absence of records, and that to have a full idea of the history of a county, the historian ideally needed to study all the parishes within that county.[33] This, of course, is a highly dubious proposition, and depends upon which parishes are studied for what purposes, but a comparative approach to localities is implicit in the argument. Interestingly, both Hoskins and Finberg were well experienced in the study of the histories of countrysides and counties, and it is clear that they understood the importance of background and context: Hoskins was at this very time completing his fine edition of the VCH for Leicestershire (edited jointly with R.A. McKinley, 1957), and he could have continued the discussion vigorously; Finberg was engaged in launching and editing *The Agrarian History of England*, and he, too, had a keen awareness of the importance of the homogeneous farming area larger than a parish.

By the end of the post-war decade and a half, however, the Leicester local historians had pinned their colours firmly to the mast, identifying themselves uncompromisingly with the local parish 'community'. Not only had they been given the title of a school, by Asa Briggs,[34] as the progenitors of a distinctive approach to their form of study, but Hoskins himself had produced a memorable *tour de force* in his book *The Midland Peasant* (1957b), which did indeed convey a clear picture of a peasant community over six centuries in the history of the parish of Wigston Magna near Leicester.

The Midland Peasant is a remarkable study of a close-knit, organically constructed and functioning agrarian village society. Cogently and clearly written, this book had all the marks of a splendid standard-setter. It had some weaknesses though: Margaret Spufford was later to criticize the author for ignoring 'spiritual man' while concentrating on the economic man;[35] and it is true that Hoskins saw his peasant community as engaged in a determined and collective struggle for survival against natural and economic forces, with landscape and environment shaping the course of the conflict. Hoskins did not devote much attention to the church as a unifying influence at the centre of the village *Gemeinschaft*, nor did he (in the book itself) make his work even more of a pioneering achievement by concentrating on the historical demography of Wigston Magna, thereby upstaging the Cambridge population campaigners by several years. However, he did publish a separate essay[36] on that subject in the same year, and was well aware that others, such as Glass, Chambers, Eversley and Habakkuk, were introducing a demographic revolution into economic and social history, a revolution with profound implications for local history.[37] Indeed, Chambers's *The Vale of Trent* was published in that year also, which was clearly a crucial year for local and regional history alike, if not actually an *annus mirabilis*.

This last characterization, admittedly extravagant-seeming, could only now serve to convey a profound sense of anti-climax. Neither Chambers nor Hoskins provoked an academic response of any breadth or weight, in the sense that in-depth studies of regions and parishes alike were slow to appear, and when the Leicester school and influence did promote important parish histories in the 1970s, these were restricted mainly to the seventeenth century.[38] The historiography of topographical and local research indicates clearly enough that the elongated or long-period study of the parish was not, in university history departments, regarded as suitable for thesis or dissertation topics. Accordingly, the idea of a small but reasonably well-defined community surviving through long phases of historical change and vicissitude was not tested out. Good local historical topic-studies continued to come from Leicester, which acquitted itself in creative and often formidably scholarly fashion in the decades that followed but, thanks to the work of Hoskins's successor (1968) in the Department, A.M. Everitt, the focus shifted to the so-called 'county community' – another mainly seventeenth-century topic – and to the patterns of distribution of English dissent. The Department had always had a deep involvement in English agrarian history in general.

This is not, however, a history of the Department of English Local History, but merely an assessment of its influential reach and incidental broad problems over a long period.[39] Although its direct academic influence was basically restricted to a growing number of faithful students and researchers (it was a postgraduate department throughout), its likely field of force was much larger, if only to the extent that many of its philosophical, educational or interpretative ideas were accepted semi-passively. To return to an argument pursued in preceding paragraphs, *The Midland Peasant* not only added lustre to the Leicester school's reputation; it gave the impression that it was practising what Hoskins and Finberg had preached, and it also very distinctly exalted the organic peasant community as the central concern of its teaching. Hoskins had made it clear that he regarded peasant society as superior, in some of its attitudes and assumptions, to the industrial society that eventually swamped the later suburb of Wigston. There was indeed a decline and a fall from 'perfection' in his story, which thereby succeeded in conveying a form of philosophical and historical idealism as central to the interpretation of a key form of pre-industrial society, in that the individual peasant reached fulfilment only within this village organism – an interpretation of the Leicester philosophy of that time more recently put forward by Christopher Parker in 1990.[40]

What the Leicester school did most comprehensively achieve was the identification of English local history with the countryside and with rural images and associations. That the identification was plausible cannot be doubted. After all, if one is tracing the story of the local 'community' through more than a millennium, then the industrializing end of that millennium must seem to be merely another and perhaps rather unwelcome stage – and of course the greater part of the story is rural, even if it takes pre-industrial towns into view, for it is well known that the latter had deep roots in the countryside. In itself this emphasis did not matter greatly, although the implicit idealist or organicist assumption did, because the latter opened itself to the charge that the Leicester scholars were not looking for conflict or division within local societies. In turn, such a limitation of vision could be methodologically crippling, since significant change within societies is often associated with friction, upheaval and structural transformation.

While it is unlikely that Hoskins would have accepted that his standpoint was organicist to this extent, the fact remains that fundamental class or social conflict did not appear in Wigston Magna, for the very good reason that that parish had no resident overlord – with the consequence that the local peasantry could run their own affairs unimpeded. Meanwhile, we have already noted the likelihood that Hoskins was rendered uncomfortable by Chambers's right-wing revisionism over enclosures; the former, after all, had represented the rich man's and the industrialist's world as the enemy, and it is necessary to re-emphasize that Hoskins was always a radical at heart. Nevertheless, it is accepted in the world of politics that radicalism can sometimes transform itself into populism, and this is what undoubtedly happened in Hoskins's case.

Very little has so far been said about the more general and public appeal of Hoskins and his colleagues at Leicester and elsewhere in promoting what can only be called open-air studies. With this general title we may subsume the largely Leicester invention of 'landscape history' with its excursions into local archaeological and agrarian fieldwork. Hoskins's own major, and now classic, study, *The Making of the English Landscape* (1955), which was in reality an inspired form of popular archaeological geography, combining the advantages of the air photography of pioneers such as O.G.S. Crawford and J.K. St Joseph with the multiple source use of a skilled and far-ranging local historian, was by far his most influential contact with a general public. Other colleagues such as Beresford, Finberg and Millward[41] made, almost simultaneously, effective public contacts with books similar in approach if more specific in subject-matter, and it is worth noticing that this type of quasi-geographical, quasi-archaeological approach still flourishes and is a major aspect of the Leicester legacy. Hoskins's chronologically elongated view of local history, it must be stressed, was closely related to his archaeological and landscape fieldwork and – in some important senses, rightly – he saw the environment as a teaching medium.

It now appears in retrospect that he could not have promoted this visual approach to localities and regions at a more propitious time. To make reference to the more immediate educational field first of all, the rapidly expanding teacher training colleges gave great stress to the study of the environment and to the use of visual aids, and it is worth noticing in this respect that both historians and geographers were enabled to develop landscape teaching in their respective spheres. Fieldwork was slowly becoming acceptable even to academically trained historians who, in any case, with the continuing growth of economic history in the universities, were adopting a wider and more comprehensive approach. Some of this new generation of teachers and students were tutoring adult classes in local as well as general history and, in a specimen adult educational region in Yorkshire, local history classes were markedly increasing.[42] More specifically, industrial archaeology became tentatively established in these years, and the muddy-boots as well as the strong-boots philosophy took hold of the archaeologically curious. As we may note, it is often erroneous to use the phrase 'historically curious'.

In the more general context of British social history (and we have to remember that Leicester local history was determinedly 'English'), the 1950s saw some broader transformations in the lives of the many; more disposable income brought rapidly increasing car ownership throughout the post-war decade[43] and, perhaps as something of a reaction from the bleakness of the immediately post-war years, there was a move towards a countryside which became more reachable. The British railway network had not then been surgically attacked, and the scope for pilgrimages increased as stately homes became more accessible, and as Britain's National Parks became established (1950–55).[44] The 1950s may well bear comparison with the late Victorian and Edwardian ages, which brought new cycling clubs and cheap travel for ramblers, and which enabled the impoverished Edward Thomas to make his literary pilgrimages. In this more recent period any form of historical nostalgia, antiquarianism or archaeology, which readily associated itself with the open air was bound to find acceptance, and in the developments of the 1950s, which included steady growth in the formation of local history societies,[45] we may find some of the more substantial roots of the present-day Heritage and popular antiquarian movement.

A great deal of the argument, from this point, turns on whether one accepts the latter development and its numerous popular centres and manifestations as historically significant and valuable. There is clearly a widespread and massive interest in physical, industrial or archaeological traces, whether the latter are interpreted through developed historical investigation or not, and it goes without saying that a skilled teacher can utilize, guide and sometimes build on this interest. But it is a professional error to underestimate the obstacles which lie in the path of such a teacher, or even of a well-meaning and determined student. Education may commence as entertainment, but it cannot remain as such if it is to leave its mark. Hoskins's books, notably his guide to topics, treatment and sources, *Local History in England* (1959), rounding off his work for that decade, set out to do more than entertain; they contained a clear wish that there should be a local historian active in every parish. This wish, too, had been expressed by W.R. Powell and R.B. Pugh. A similar sentiment was embodied in yet another popular 1950s guide to local history, the handbook *Teach Yourself Local History* (1958) by Francis Celoria, 'written by a layman for laymen'. This, more than the other guides, stressed the work and importance of the well-organized and non-antiquarian local history society, and preached a form of enlightened self-help and mutual help. The author in this case was the then (1955–58) Secretary of the Hampstead Local History Society, and his book was exceptional in that it catered for the townsperson and in that it gave a wide range of references and made reference to unusual topics such as folklore and sociology.

Both Hoskins and Celoria, in the midst of a plethora of informed advice about research and reading, included archaeological topics and material. However, it is an unfortunate fact that archaeology, a highly organized group of techniques and form of investigation which is most apposite or effective when documentary information is scarce or missing, makes an appearance in local historical research mainly when a very convergent and specific form of study is in train. Since it deals with highly particularized topics (a given building, a site of interest), and very specific physical traces relating to the latter, it can soon snare the student who is antiquarian-minded – and who is thereby apt to forget that history is about life in general and its manifold problems. Hoskins, who disliked antiquarianism, was certainly keenly aware of this danger, but his own passion for fieldwork was even stronger and was often expressed in writing in the 1950s and 1960s.[46] Hoskins, too, was aware of the gap between the professional historian and the leisure-time amateur, just as he had a shrewd idea of the likely interests and limitations of the latter, and he did not delude himself with the notion that major and original works of interpretation would be forthcoming from the amateurs of Britain. Indeed, he suggested in the first edition of *Local History in England* that the student or reader would be well occupied in carefully collecting material for the likely use of the VCH volumes –

and it is clear that he did not see a major independent role for the private and non-professional researcher.

In particular, Hoskins did not recommend the study of modern urban or industrial history in a local setting. In this, he remained true to the message of *The Midland Peasant*, which ended its tale when industrial buildings began to appear in local fields. Through the developments here described there runs what is, to the educationally aspirant of an older generation, a depressing story of an historical retreat, the abandonment of the original high aims of the adult education movement, designed to equip the citizen of the modern world with the best that part-time higher education could offer. The historical message of R.H. Tawney's classes in Edwardian England, aimed at the sharpest intellectual rigour, was very different from that of the local-history-for-amusement that had appeared by the middle of the century.[47] Yet Hoskins could quite reasonably dedicate *The Midland Peasant* to Tawney and, of course, the former was very much on the side of the person who wished to improve himself or herself.

If Hoskins had wistfully hoped that a people's history movement might appear, then he was not alone. The earliest academic contributors to the *Amateur Historian* magazine, founded in 1952, included a succession of prominent (and later eminent) members of the then Historians' Group of the Communist Party,[48] who evidently wished to see the growth of a popular, rather than populist, movement in which people in localities would write their own collective histories, democratically triumphant over the Cold War. This same spirit and sentiment made a rather more than fitful appearance in the History Workshop movement in the 1970s, and it has become firmly lodged in the project work espoused since 1972 by the Oral History Society. Yet it remains true that these movements, worthy though they are, hardly touch the problems that British local history now faces. Labour and feminist history have tended to stay in the hands of rather insular devotees, who are all too often unconcerned about locality, place, broader social context and background. The struggle takes place without more than a formal frame, or within the terms of an immediate situation.

British local history has not changed fundamentally since those formative days of the 1950s. The few professionals seek to set examples which may touch colleagues, but are otherwise limited in their influence. There is a more experienced and adaptable professional stratum, but it has few keen debates, having become institutionalized, and until the arrival of the crushingly unfavourable conditions of the 1990s it had relied too heavily on the incidental usefulness of the subject to many historians. In other words, it has only begun to create a distinctive identity for itself outside Leicester. Regional history, on the other hand, has become formally and even vigorously established in a number of centres, but has suffered from specialist narrowness and lack of definition. Local history has remained steadily popular as a subject in adult education, but the threats to the latter have thrown a vast responsibility on to the local history societies, which have never given real proof that they can make its pursuit more than an absorbing and fragmented recreation.

Yet there are signs of hope. The latter, however, cannot offer advantage until worrying aspects of the world of local history are fairly examined. There has so far been not a little self-delusion in this story, and the real problems facing the subject are usually avoided as unpleasant, embarrassing and inconvenient. One of these, fragmentation of subject-matter, is discussed in the next chapter.

Notes

1. Phythian-Adams, C. (1987), *Rethinking Local History*, Department of English Local History Occasional Paper, Fourth Series, No. 1, first edn, University of Leicester Press, Leicester, is the only such statement to be published in recent years. But see the references to Finberg, nn 24, 29 and 32 below.

2. Levine, P. (1986), *The Amateur and the Professional: Antiquarians, Historians and Archeologists in Victorian England, 1838–1866*, Cambridge University Press: Cambridge.

3. Even a particularly erudite and unpretentious recent guide, Tiller, K. (1992), *English Local History: An Introduction*, Alan Sutton: Stroud, risks confusion by using 'history' in this way in its opening chapter, although at one point (p. 12) the author circumvents the problem by referring to 'antiquarian histories'.

4. Hoskins, W.G. (1966), *English Local History: The Past and the Future*, pamphlet, University of Leicester Press, Leicester, inaugural lecture given at the University, 3 March, 5.

5. A relative of the writer spent much time trying to show that his branch of the family were somehow descended from the Dukes of Leeds – because of the accident of a common surname (Osborn). This type of aspiration is more common among the antiquarian-minded than among historians.

6. For example, Hudson, P. (1992), 'Land, the Social Structure and Industry in Two Yorkshire Townships, 1660–1800' in P. Swan, and D. Foster (eds), *Essays in Regional and Local History*, Hutton Press: Beverley, esp. pp. 27–8, where strength of 'manorialisation' is brought out as a relevant factor.

7. Phythian-Adams (1987), 37–40.

8. That a form of social history can be extracted from modern county administrations is demonstrated in Lee J.M. (1963), *Social Leaders and Public Persons*, Manchester University Press: Manchester.

9. Cf. Lee, C.H. (1971), *Regional Economic Growth in the United Kingdom since the 1880s*, McGraw-Hill: London and New York; *idem* (1980),

'Regional Structural Change in the Long Run: Britain, 1841–1971', in S. Pollard (ed.), *Region und Industrialisierung*, Vandenhoeck and Ruprecht: Göttingen, both *passim* for the use of county areas.

10. See Thomas, E. (1985), in M. Justin Davis, (ed.), *A Literary Pilgrim; an Illustrated Guide to Britain's Literary Heritage*, Exeter. This collection was first published in 1917. But cf. Howkins, A. (1986), 'The Discovery of Rural England' in R. Colls and P. Dodd, (eds), *Englishness, Politics and Culture, 1880–1920*, Croom Helm: Brighton and London.

11. Regional novelists of this century like Graham Sutton (Cumberland) and Crichton Porteous (Derbyshire) have plainly used considerable local historical information. For a consideration of regional literature in general, see Butlin, R.A. (1990), 'Regions in England and Wales, *c*. 1600–1914' in R.A. Dodgshon and R.A. Butlin, *An Historical Geography of England and Wales*, 2nd edn, Academic Press: London, 246–50.

12. Editorial by Fitzhugh, T. (1952) in *Amateur Historian*, 1, (1), August–September.

13. Cf. the classic opening shots of this campaign, as set forth in Clapham, J.H. (1930), *An Economic History of Modern Britain*, vol. 1, 2nd edn, Cambridge University Press: Cambridge, preface, ix–x.

14. For the charged atmosphere, cf. Fieldhouse, R. (1985a), *Adult Education and the Cold War: Academic Values under Siege 1946–51*, pamphlet, University of Leeds: Leeds; *idem* (1985b), 'Conformity and Confrontation in English Responsible Body Adult Education, 1925–50', *Studies in the Education of Adults*, 17, (2). The writer in any case lived through, in the 1950s, the type of situation described.

15. Chambers, J.D. (1932), *Nottinghamshire in the Eighteenth Century*, P.S. King: London, preface, vi. But cf. also the parallel comments in Phythian-Adams, (1987), 1–2.

16. Phythian-Adams (1987) rightly points out that Tupling was writing, in Rossendale, with an eye on national economic history, but the latter stayed faithful to local and Lancashire history. Cf. his memorial and bibliography (1962) in *Transactions of the Antiquarian Society of Lancashire and Cheshire*, 72, pp. 177–9. The full details of the works mentioned in this paragraph are: Tupling, G.H. (1927), *The Economic History of Rossendale*, publications of the University of Manchester Economic History Series, IV, Manchester University Press: Manchester; Heaton, H. (1920), *The Yorkshire Woollen and Worsted Industry*, Oxford Historical and Literary Studies, 10, Clarendon Press: Oxford; Daniels, G.W. (1920), *The Early English Cotton Industry, with some Unpublished Letters of Samuel Crompton*, University of Manchester Historical Series, 36, Manchester University Press: Manchester; Court, W.H.B. (1938), *The Rise of the Midland Industries, 1600–1838*, Oxford University Press: Oxford; Dodd, A.H. (1933), *The Industrial Revolution in North Wales*, University of Wales Press Board: Cardiff.

17. *The Vale of Trent* was published as a separate paper in 1957 by Cambridge University Press at Cambridge, as the *Economic History Review*, Supplement No. 3.

18. Chambers (1932).

19. Hoskins, W.G. (1937), 'The Fields of Wigston Magna', *Transactions of the Leicester Archaeological Society* (hereafter *TLAS*), 19, 163–9.

20. Information by courtesy of Professor M.W. Beresford.

21. Finberg, H.P.R. (1967), 'The Local Historian and his Theme', essay reprinted in H.P.R. Finberg, and V.H.T. Skipp, *Local History: Objective and Pursuit*, David and Charles: Newton Abbot, 10.

22. Ibid. See also H.P.R. Finberg (1962), 'Local History' in H.P.R. Finberg, (ed.), *Approaches to History*, Routledge: London, 117.

23. Stacey, M. (1969), 'The Myth of Community Studies', *British Journal of Sociology*, 20, 134–47.

24. Finberg, (1962), 121.

25. Chambers, J.D. (1953), 'Enclosure and Labour Supply in the Industrial Revolution', *Economic History Review*, V, reprinted in D.V. Glass and D.E.C. Eversley (1965) *Population in History*, Arnold: London.

26. Crafts, N.F.R. (1978), 'Enclosure and Labour Supply Revisited', *Explorations in Economic History*, XV, but in particular Snell, K.D.M (1985), *Annals of the Labouring Poor: Social Change and Agrarian England, 1660–1900*, Cambridge University Press: Cambridge, 138–227, which surveys a mass of relevant literature on the subject.

27. Chambers and Hoskins were close acquaintances through residential proximity during 1946–51 (in Nottingham and Leicester respectively), and Hoskins of course knew the drift of Chambers's arguments – and did not agree with them regarding enclosures (personal note by the author). In any case, as Snell (1985, pp. 281–2) points out Chambers contradicted his earlier view of enclosures as expressed in *Nottinghamshire in the Eighteenth Century*, 179–82.

28. Fieldhouse (1985a and b), *passim*.

29. Finberg (1962), 116.

30. Hoskins, W.G. (1952), 'The Writing of Local History', *History Today*, 2, (1), 491.

31. Powell, W.R. (1958), 'Local History in Theory and Practice', *Bulletin of the Institute of Historical Research*, 31, 41–8.

32. Finberg (1962), 121.

33. Powell (1958), 44–5.

34. Briggs, A. (1958), review, 'The Leicester School', *New Statesman and Nation*, 15 February 1958, 206–7. The reviewer praises what is here christened 'The Leicester School', but also draws attention to the latter's lack of interest in the modern world.

35. Spufford, M. (1973), 'The Total History of Village Communities', *Local Historian*, 10, (8), November, 399.

36. Hoskins, W.G. (1957a), 'The Population of an English Village, 1086–1801' in *TLAS.*, 33, 15–35. This is Hoskins's separate account of demographic change in Wigston Magna.

37. Eversley, D.E.C., Laslett, P. and Wrigley E.A. (eds) (1966), *An Introduction to English Historical Demography*, Weidenfeld and Nicolson: London, has valuable evidence on the pre-Cambridge development of population study in localities, especially in the Bibliography, 241ff.

38. The most outstanding examples in this genre are: Spufford, M. (1974), *Contrasting Communities: English Villagers in the Sixteenth and Seventeen Centuries*, Cambridge University Press: Cambridge; Hey, D.G. (1974), *An English Rural Community: Myddle under the Tudors and Stuarts*, Leicester University Press: Leicester; and Wrightson, K. and Levine, D. (1978), *Poverty and Piety in an English Village, 1525–1700*, Cambridge University Press: Cambridge; also, by the same authors, (1991), *The*

Making of an Industrial Society, Whickham, 1560-1765, Oxford University Press: Oxford. Howell, C. (1983), *Land, Family and Inheritance in Transition: Kibworth Harcourt, 1280–1700*, Leicester University Press: Leicester, is one of the few local studies to link medieval and early modern local history.

39.   A most valuable survey of the work of the Department of English Local History is to be found in Everitt, A.M. and Tranter, M. (1978), *Local History at Leicester, 1948–1978: A Bibliography of Writings by Members of the Department of English Local History*, University of Leicester: Leicester.

40.   Cf. Parker, C. (1990), *The English Historical Tradition*, John Donald: Edinburgh, 234–6. For an assessment of Hoskins, see Phythian-Adams, C. (1992), 'Hoskins's England: A Local Historian of Genius and the Realisation of his Theme', *Local Historian*, 22, (4), November. 170–83, esp. 176–8. This study of Hoskins, based partly on his private thoughts, shows that the latter's idealist approach to the English (or Midland) peasantry was formed by 1944–45. Hoskins had a detestation of many aspects of present-day civilization, which he described as 'money-ridden' and 'town-minded'. As will easily be seen, this opened Hoskins to the charge of encouraging escapism.

41.   These volumes here concerned are: Beresford, M.W. (1954), *The Lost Villages of England*, Lutterworth Press: London; Finberg, H.P.R. (1955), *Gloucestershire: the History of the Landscape*, Hodder and Stoughton: London; and Millward, R. (1955), *Lancashire: the History of the Landscape*, Hodder and Stoughton: London. This genre of volume enjoyed another wave of popularity in the 1970s, when most of the counties of England were covered by individual authors. For a bibliography of landscape history, see Knowles, C.H. (*c.* 1983), *Landscape History*, Historical Association.

42.   Cf. Noble, M. and Crowther, J. (1992), 'Adult Education and the Development of Regional and Local History: East Yorkshire and North Lincolnshire, c.1929–1985', in P. Swan and D. Foster (eds), *Essays in Regional and Local History*, Hutton Press: Beverley, 150–70, and especially 154–5.

43.   Perkin, H. (1976), *The Age of the Automobile*, Quarter Books: London, 206: there was a rapid surge of car ownership in the early 1950s.

44.   Ibid., 165–9; also Hewison, R. (1987), *The Heritage Industry*, Methuen: London, 63.

45.   Report of the Committee to Review Local History (The Blake Committee), (1979), issued on behalf of the Standing Conference for Local History, London, 9–10, with diagrams.

46.   Examples of Hoskins's commitment to fieldwork are: Hoskins, W.G. (1956), 'Fieldwork in Local History', *Amateur Historian*, 3, (1), Autumn; *idem* (1967) *Fieldwork in Local History*, Faber: London. Such statements apart, his general activities supported his philosophy.

47.   Harrison, J.F.C. (1961), *Learning and Living, 1790–1960*, Routledge: London, gives a vivid picture of the general transformation that overtook adult education in the post-1945 years (especially pp. 318–19 and 332 ff. One has the impression that the author is describing the onset of a consumer society and, of course, local history was one of the commodities sold.

48.   The historians here contributing included Hill, Hobsbawm, Rudé, Dorothy Thompson, Hilton, Saville and Morton. For the group as a whole, see Kaye, H.J. (1984), *The British Marxist Historians*, Cambridge University Press: Cambridge.

CHAPTER TWO

Local History and the Fragmentation Impasse

Local history in Britain is in a largely unrecognized impasse, produced by a fragmentation of subject-matter in all branches of history. This trend is wholly reflective of the increasing output of publications, theses and dissertations in all areas of learning, and it is so much a part of the lives of academics that it goes almost unnoticed in the midst of the steadily increasing pressures placed on the individual throughout the field of tertiary education.

Since this trend and these pressures are universal, why should local history be singled out for special attention? What is the real significance of the term 'fragmentation'? To attempt to answer the first question, the various forms of local or localized history (and, as has been indicated, the latter adjective has its uses), like urban or sub-regional history, are not specialisms as that word is commonly understood; they are amalgams of a variety of developing specialisms, skills and standpoints, brought together with a view to illuminating the development of a locality. It can now be said that the idea of a local historian as one who goes straight to documents with the aim of tracing the development of a village 'community' is an over-simplified and restricting view, which largely ignores the major national upheavals of the last two centuries.[1] Local history also reaches out to thousands of part-time students, and has a recognized educational function in intra-mural tertiary education, as well as in adult class, school and local history society. These points were made clearly enough by the Blake Committee of 1977–79.[2] The last mentioned body, however, tended in practice to treat local history as a homogeneous commodity made available for consumers, which of course it is not, and any factor or group of factors which complicates such history as a study must of necessity touch all those who teach or study it. The Committee also showed itself to be properly concerned about the provision of 'access to training' in the subject and, in the decade and a half that has elapsed since the former deliberated, there has been a considerable expansion of part-time training for adults in research techniques for the local historian.[3]

It should be evident that training, whether of adults or youthful undergraduates, must keep up with developments in the subject. At one time it was apparently thought sufficient to reproduce such guidance as came from the Leicester scholars,[4] but the advent of local history certificates and diplomas has brought more attention to urban and rudimentary 'regional' (i.e. county) history, the latter forms having enjoyed some promotion in British universities since the mid-1960s.[5] In other words, local history has moved beyond its rural and semi-archaeological image and fixation and, as will be shown, it is now receiving challenges thrown out by specialisms which develop constantly around it. Some of these challenges, it is fair to say, come from present-day Leicester scholars,[6] who have certainly not allowed their thinking to remain static since the days of Finberg and Hoskins. The main stimuli, however, have come from existing fields of historical interest which have developed because of their acknowledged importance to historians in general. These fields reach across a considerable range of historical preoccupations: seventeenth-century political and social studies of the gentry which have found uses for regional or county data, the study of religious sentiment and control in a similar period (as exemplified in Spufford, 1974), a developing historical demography which has drawn heavily on local material, a body of agrarian history which has some multiplying ramifications and a very substantial local base, and the development of increasingly probing and sometimes complex studies of the growth of early industries in the countryside.[7]

Some of these branches of study have been willingly absorbed by local historians. Indeed, local historical demography was received with enthusiasm in the middle and late 1960s although, as we may note, local history's powers of assimilation and adaptation have tended to be weak. The Leicester Department was deeply involved in the promotion of agrarian history from its earliest independent stage, and was, as we have seen, responsible for the successive volumes of *The Agrarian History of England* – thus, incidentally, fixating local history even more solidly in the countryside. Landscape history, having been virtually created by Leicester pioneers,[8] became itself a minor specialism, at once a set of visual aids and a teaching technique. Most of the foregoing instances, meanwhile, relate to fundamental forms of subject-matter, not all of which have been easy to assimilate into local historical methodology and practice. Yet it is the strength and the weakness of local history that it is, or must sooner or later be, *microcosmic*; it reflects and even concentrates much wider movements and realities in regional or national life. Finberg went so far as to assert that 'there are towns which, despite their modest size, have exhibited in a state of high perfection the most characteristic elements of our economic, religious, parliamentary and civic history'.[9]

There is even more to the matter than this, for a modest parish will 'exhibit' many of the characteristics of its surrounding region, and if we then abandon the parish and examine its 'social area' (or general meet-ing territory for inhabitants and members of families),[10] we shall be struck by the realization that this area *was* the nation, for much of the time, for a large group of the parish-dwellers themselves. It is the countryside or town district in which they have spent by far the greatest part of their lives. The singularity – and also the representativeness – of their individual and collective existences is there, lending immense im-portance to the local history of such an area, and making more general historical disquisitions seem like empty generalization, intellectual con-test and vanity. It was this sentiment, a dangerous one, that caused Hoskins to quote William Blake's assertion, that 'to Generalize is to be an Idiot. To Particularize is the Alone Distinction of Merit'.[11]

If local or localized history can claim this degree of importance, then it cannot afford to ignore the developing insights, growing subtleties and expanding learning within the great body of historical study, and it must be prepared to use any intellectual or methodological safe-break-ing equipment that is available for use. Most enthusiastic devotees of the subject, who are at the same time concerned with rather more than collecting, will undoubtedly agree with this proposition. Nevertheless, they must be prepared to look fearlessly at what is now involved, for developing and inexorable specialization has now taken hold of almost every branch of history, to the extent that there currently seems to be a specialism for every one of a hundred small groups of historians now writing and publishing. Many of these specialisms, fortunately or unfor-tunately, have some bearing on that very important local area of the nation which was mentioned in the previous paragraph. Accordingly, the significance of the term 'fragmentation' will immediately become somewhat clearer.

The reader, moreover, should not despair at the immense and vari-egated heap of sophisticated information that he or she appears to be expected to control and to synthesize. What is urged in this book is a degree of tough-mindedness, an element of resistance to misleading sales talk about local history, one that is not customarily invoked in discussions on the subject, and all that is ultimately required is a sense of realism as well as a saving determination. Meanwhile, the local historian is only drowned in information if he or she has no ideas to act as life-saving equipment, and he or she has been singularly deprived of themes and schemes, through the use of which the investigator can tease out what is quite genuinely and palpably the history of a locality or a district – and can do so without finding that he or she is, after all, sitting on a heap of mere fragments.

The student may be reassured to find that the general problem of fragmentation is one afflicting history generally. Unfortunately, local or urban or regional history pose problems of synthesis, the act of bringing together a multitude of elements and pieces of specialist information, that most historians face only if they are writers of general textbooks – with the incidental qualification that the task of the localist is more difficult in that he or she is using original sources as well as a variety of methodologies and interpretative ideas. Let us, in the meantime, detail some of the fragmenting specialisms which surround local history.

To survey the specialized systems of knowledge and enquiry which operate within the body of general history (and which bear down on the localist, all taking varying forms according to historical period): these systems or special fields have to do with Parliament, the law and national administration, military affairs, a catalogue of economic and social institutions like poor law bodies, friendly societies and banks, another possible catalogue of minor and major industries and their practices and technologies, a massive and often intractable body of information on the subject of transport, yet another on farming's local and regional practices, much relatively elusive material on wages and labour conditions, some very ill-organized special information on the very important subject of the building industry, a plethora of antiquarian details relating to all forms of architecture, much cramping and repetitive information from local records of administration (usually given considerable prominence in guides to the pursuit of local history),[12] and a mass of discussion on the supposed organization of society and on patterns of life and culture from social historians, oral historians and demographers. Since the local historian's work is ostensibly concerned with matters relating to folklife and tradition, he or she may be alarmed to find that there appears to be no real communication between the folklorists on the one hand, and social historians on the other.[13]

This is typical of many historical specialisms. They commence with a heady search for new insights, and descend thereafter through degrees of inward-lookingness as their organization of discussion and knowledge becomes established over time. However, specialist organization within history varies, and a brief outline of the evolution of some main specialisms (all of importance to local history) is given below. Meanwhile, the idea of fragmentation itself calls for more clarification. The latter is not merely the product of the division or breaking of history into subject topics – these are unavoidable and seem to arise from growing consensus between historians. The real problem resides in the apparent incompatibility of methodologies and preoccupations as between subject specialisms, leading to almost total non-communication between the devotees of one specialist field and those of another. The localist occupies a sensitive position that sooner or later impels him or her to observe these incompatibilities; others may not so readily notice.

Another form of fragmentation is that arising not so much from multi-plication of subject topics as such (although that may certainly take place over time), as an increase in the numbers of specialist papers within certain general areas, many of them on very minor topics which make them antiquarian in spirit and nature. This is a problem that arises when an accepted specialism (such as agrarian history) touches on highly specific archaeological territory.

Here we come to one of the greatest incompatibilities of all, the divide – at the local level – between two great systems of historical knowledge, archaeology and history. From this division much fragmentation derives. As had been noted, W.G. Hoskins made sure that a measure of archaeology was inserted into the study of local history, not only by recommending the study of, say, local and vernacular architecture, but by virtue of the long-period approach to small localities, which went very well both with that scholar's advocacy of fieldwork and with a 'landscape' or quasi-archaeological approach to countrysides. It is not here suggested that field evidence, or that of archaeology in general, should be ignored. This is most certainly not advocated. The problem is a procedural and psychological one, one that lies in the truth that local archaeology is for practical purposes descriptive, while history is analytical and synthesizing.

On a broader front, the compatibilities between history and archaeology are more evident, and an impressive case for a *rapprochement* between the two has been made by Dymond.[14] Hence, archaeological material, surveyed over regions and countrysides, can be made to yield important generalizations, and Hoskins's attempt to date and characterize 'the Great Rebuilding' is a case in point, as is Machin's qualifying response.[15] However, such significant generalization – very far from idiocy! – is rarely produced in small-area local histories, which have to deal with restricted samples, and enquiries of this kind really belong to regional architectural and cultural studies, or to surveys of major towns and cities. Those who wish to record, exactly and carefully, at the local level should not be denied their chance to do so, and there is a strong case for combining such efforts in regional teams. However, this is a specifically organizational matter and does not alter the force of the point that is made here,

Detailed archaeological description has two major drawbacks: first, it is frequently incompatible with the development of historical argument, being concerned with a mass of items of observed fact which relate to a highly distinctive frame of reference, be the latter some aspect of the historic study of architecture or earth traces or some branch of technology. Second, it encourages, by virtue of such absorptions, a continuing antiquarian cast of mind. The student (and observed instances abound) may undertake this work because of initial predilections, but it is educationally and historically damaging to leave him or her in a state whereby they are incapable of anything but description of the discrete. The main remedy is to remind students (and some teachers) that artefacts are produced by human beings in a given situation, and that the former gain in value from increases in historical knowledge surrounding them.

The real test of post-medieval and modern archaeology, including the industrial variety, is 'does it help significantly in the posing of historical questions which might otherwise have been ignored had the archaeological evidence not been available?' These popular branches of study are passing through an intensely particularizing phase, whereby the identification of technological antecedents and meticulous site description (not bad things in themselves) take priority over all broader historical considerations.[16] The most serious criticism of industrial archaeology ('IA') devotees, sadly, is the common one directed against dyed-in-the-wool antiquaries. They forget the man or woman who made or operated the device under examination. As Samuel remarked, 'the workplace is lovingly reconstructed, but the workers themselves can remain mere shadows, dwarfed by the physical setting'.[17]

Industrial archaeology is now pursued by specialist study groups and by local historians throughout the country. What has happened as a result is that hundreds of local history societies have assorted and fragmented details of industries which have left traces in their territories. Very often this information has been left in a vacuum, because the groups concerned have been unable to bring the details together in any wider discourse. Yet this immediate outcome is not a surprising one; industrial archaeology embraces a mass of specific types of industry and artefact, so much so that when the writer had to construct, some years ago, a photographic index relating to the industries in a given region, he found himself with over a hundred separate class-headings for industries and handicrafts in the area concerned. It would be pleasant to think that historical perceptions were sharpened and strengthened by this great accession of knowledge, but the accumulation of technical and other details does not necessarily bring wisdom. Here we see both accumulation and fragmentation in particularly striking form, whereby disparate items of all kinds jostle one with the other, their value apparently derived not from historical context but from physical appearance in sites as curios and scarcely more. Some generalizations will have been made possible, but only by a labour that tends to produce the repetitive or the blindingly obvious.

Industrial archaeology was, like several important specialisms, essentially an outgrowth from the main or stem specialism of economic history. Its first stirrings belong mainly to the out-of-doors phase of the

1950s, previously described, and are associated with the late Michael Rix.[18] It is customary for special-interest groups to form themselves around a journal or in a society, and the first in chronology and precedence was the Agricultural History Society, founded with special support from Leicester and Reading Universities in 1953. Finberg became first editor of the *Agricultural History Review* in the same year, and the Department of English Local History was deeply committed to this new main specialism of economic history, Joan Thirsk having been appointed as Research Fellow in Agrarian History in 1950.[19] However, the achievements of these scholars are well known. To pursue our thesis further, it is fascinating to see how a specialism takes over, and sometimes transmutes and also fragments the subject-matter within its area.

What emerged – and only a small proportion of this output appeared in the *Agricultural History Review* – was a predictable mixture of individual topics, all of interest to somebody, and ranging from fen drainage, the architecture of farmhouses, forestry, the study of individual manors, feudal rents, field names, farmhouse inventories, plough marks and patterns, and crop nutrition, to deserted villages and wool price fluctuations.[20] Many of these were of obvious interest to local historians, and in addition there was some clearly valuable work on the regional development of farming, notably by such authorities as Hoskins and Fussell. A decade after the formation of the Agricultural History Society, a survey of 'Work in Progress'[21] in the same sphere revealed some common interests among large groups and some areas of deep concentration. There was, indeed, considerable survey work on regions, much of it by geographers, but even more work (about a third in all) was archaeological in drift or specifically local – 'ridge and furrow in Bedfordshire and Oxfordshire' has to be classed as archaeological, even though a survey of this kind will yield valuable generalizations. There were unifying trends: scholars and students from seven or eight different types of department were working in this amorphous yet extensive territory. Other data (see note 20) show that agricultural or agrarian history was attracting as much attention through publications as was the specifically local variety. Meanwhile, only a handful seemed to be debating anything that was controversial (the consequences of enclosure had attracted two persons out of 165 listed) and excursions into major agrarian, political and social movements were restricted to a few well-known historians.

Fragmentation is a psychological state quite as much as a disorganizational process, and perhaps the most significant commentary on this major outgrowth of economic history was that, after agricultural history had been encouraging group concerns for more than a generation, a new and far more broadly interested journal, *Rural His-*

tory; Economy, Society, Culture (1991), had to attempt to introduce vigorous debate into the same area. Agricultural history had been largely a holdall for a multiplicity of topics, most of them of technical interest only, and a few of the latter had any impact on the body of history as a whole. Local history gained some usable regional background, much confusing technology and a scattering of highly specific or archaeologically biased articles.

Agricultural history attracted the dutiful attention of fair numbers of economic historians, as did another parallel study, transport history (which found expression in the Leicester-based *Journal of Transport History,* 1953) and in the more particularizing and antiquarian-leaning Railway and Canal Historical Society. Although many economic historians encouraged the study of the economic effects of transport, the latter topic was rarely incorporated into local studies as a key theme.[22] The late 1950s and early 1960s saw the emergence of two more broad-seeming but in fact highly specific fields of group involvement, which few local historians seemed able to assess – perhaps because both had nineteenth- and twentieth-century urban emphases, when local history was looking to the countryside of earlier periods. These were business history (the journal *Business History* was founded in 1958) and labour history (the Society for the Study of Labour History was established in 1960). T.S. Ashton, in launching *Business History,* drew attention to the diversification of subject-matter in economic history: 'no single journal can meet the needs of all; and hence recently, separate publications have appeared to treat of transport, agriculture and other specialisms'.[23]

Samuel later wrote tellingly on the limitations of business history from a localist's point of view – if we accept his implication that the purpose of a local historian is to approach more closely to human beings in their various degrees and life situations. Business records, he argued,

> tell us more about the marketing of goods than about the people who made them (or who sold them), more about wages than about work (even wage books are comparative rarities); ledgers and day books make it comparatively easy to write about growth and consolidation while giving no indication at all about fissiparous tendencies working in the opposite direction, family rivalries, for instance, scheming managers, or partners who took to the bottle ...[24]

Unfortunately, Samuel did not stress that the study of business operations is of vital importance in that these latter react, sometimes unfavourably, on local populations, and that the history of decision-making is of concern to localities and to the education of their citizens. Labour history, for its part, was certainly concerned with human beings pro-

vided that they belonged to the *dramatis personae* of labour organizations, and its greatest omission – still only partly rectified – was a
failure to take an interest in the setting of the drama itself, the locality
in which labour struggles were enacted. In the case of labour historians,
there was undoubtedly a supposition that class should be more important than place, and this assumption was probably sharpened by a
dislike of the notion of 'community', with its partly hidden acceptance
of social equilibrium. The result was that much labour history was
abstracted from its surroundings, as indeed was business history. Sidney
Pollard's fine *A History of Labour in Sheffield* (1959), with its thorough
analysis of background, gave the labour historians less excuse for their
omissions than they might otherwise have had. Business historians rarely
or never looked at the local connections and compositions of labour
forces. They preferred to pursue policy descriptions and to travel more
widely than the mere locality.

Abstraction of this kind, which ignores place and the characteristics
of situation, has undoubtedly held back the more perceptive study of
localities. We shall examine the role of place later on. There are few, if
any, instances whereby business and labour historians have co-operated
in writing the history of a modern town, even though such a study
would be invigorating. The town historian is in any case too often
prone to have recourse to the more arid records of local government.
Fragmentation, meanwhile, is not restricted to incompatibilities of subject-matter or to non-communication between specialisms, flagrant as
these may sometimes appear to be. It is a product of the sheer volume of
published material within all of the categories so far mentioned, and
within others still to be mentioned.

The most important specialism – within local history – to take shape
in this period was that of local population study, promoted by the
Cambridge Group for the Study of Population and Social Structure
during 1963–64. This appeared to offer an immense amount to students
of localities, and volunteers from all over England and Wales co-operated with the Cambridge pioneers in aggregating parish register entries.[25] It had already been understood by early workers in this field that
analysis of such entries provided a vertebrate element in local history,[26]
in that they gave information about changing populations seen as a
whole, and the advent of family reconstitution in Britain (1965–67)
provided insights into the 'community'. The Cambridge organizers,
then, commenced with excellent intentions, recommending the collection of parish data for subsequent analysis, and plainly intending to
study the main characteristics of British parishes comparatively.[27] But it
soon became clear that despite their large-scale and exciting use of local
data, they were primarily and understandably concerned with questions

of national and international demography; the local material was used instrumentally. Here is a perfectly clear example of instrumentality at work.

The Cambridge organizers gave local historical demography a set of aims and purposes, above and distinct from the illumination of the individual locality *per se*, and these aims were enthusiastically taken up by the Local Population Studies Society (1968). Particular localities, Colyton being the best-known case, were indeed studied in depth (Shepshed, Bottesford and, more recently, Havering in Essex are other examples), but few were examined exhaustively in this way, and even Colyton had to wait for many years before the economic history of its neighbourhood was extensively followed up.[28] The local demographer can retort that it is the task of other local historians to provide a richer and a deeper background in such cases, but much also depends on the aims and organization of serious study in any one place, and there is a point at which the growth and influence of a highly skilled and well-organized specialism such as local population study becomes inhibiting to other forms of investigation, and thereby restrictive. The specialism itself loses by not making linkages in many directions. Far more attention needs to be given to local projects which bring disciplines and techniques together.

The fact remains that local population study provides an excellent basis for a widening investigation relating numbers of variables, like village type, patterns of occupation, economic development, class and social structure, forms of agriculture, food supplies and diet, climate, famine, price movements and a host of similar factors, most of which have to be studied in regional terms. However, the Cambridge Group felt unable to develop regional surveys in view of a need to concentrate on the national demographic picture.[29] The local historian, more than ever tied to the parish and its registers, was left with yet more fragments, pieces of population data which he or she could not satisfactorily explain in local or regional terms. Yet the same student has also incurred a very real debt to the population specialists, whose activities have opened many windows.

The early 1970s brought two other major developments, the establishment of social history (1975) as an interest and organization separate from that of the economic stem, and oral history (1971), which was principally a technique of collecting information from living human beings, an approach in turn dependent on the availability of the cheap tape recorder. Oral collection has had as much significance for local history as has the social variety. Oral history has seemingly opened the way into the heart, mind and world of the common man or woman, and it was quickly regarded by members of the growing Oral History

Society as a new form of people's history. The hopes and aspirations of the eminent Marxist contributors to the early *Amateur Historian* of the 1950s now seemed to be realized. The experiences of workshop, working-class terrace and industrial city and environment would be on hand in great quantity, with raw material from neglected areas of every kind. This would be history written from below, and Raphael Samuel, in a noteworthy essay, accordingly gave a local historical lead to the newly formed (1976) History Workshop.[30]

For a few years this movement showed very real promise. In the end it was defeated, temporarily at least, by the fact that labour or labour-inclined historians are not happy with the idea of place as a conditioning factor both on the testimonies of oral history and on the chemistry of broader movements. Additionally, there is virtually no imaginative background history, in readiness for the oral historians to use, within twentieth-century towns. Studies like Savage's (1987) *The Dynamics of Working-Class Politics*, an account of the development of Preston as a background to a close analysis of labour strategies and campaign approaches, are exceedingly rare, and one is reminded that such history has never touched the conservative world of county local history committees and federations, nor has it reached out to local history societies – which in reality need the stimulus of such ideas. The History Workshop movement (1976–80) produced some thoughtful debates on the nature of local history, as well as a number of instructive local projects,[31] and past discussions may indeed re-emerge and develop as young historians face the problems of locality study (see Chapter 7).

Social history, through the Social History Society, produced the ultimate form of fragmentation by separating the social from the economic. That it gave scores of historians a sense of liberation from conventional studies of economic fluctuation cannot be doubted, and it opened up great new areas of subject-matter touching on cultural and social organizations, on the structure of society and of groups, on patterns of population, on professionalization, and on class in society and a mass of related topics. Like other groups, it realized that it would have to exploit local material in an instrumentalist fashion, but its direct impact on local or 'community' history was not great – and was represented by the ingenious work of Alan Macfarlane and associates in the guide *Reconstructing Historical Communities* (1977a), arguing in effect for total record linkage. For Macfarlane, however, the parish is a 'community', and he says little or nothing about the history of the last 200 years. His computer-based record analysis concentrated mainly on the sixteenth and seventeenth centuries, thus appealing to the document-centred local history which has rested heavily on that period. The fine work of Levine and Wrightson has shown how the local history of that age can be synthesized, and built round important themes in social history, but it has so far influenced broader local historical practice only in passing. For the relevant debates in the local historical field have not sited themselves centrally in the historical spectrum at all: the Levine and Wrightson studies are addressed to social historians, and the History Workshop debate had its own distinct and only partly central audience of young and radical historians, whose discussions stayed inside their own ranks.

In other words, divisions of gender, social grouping, fashion and also class contributed to the prevailing and by now unstoppable fragment-ations, many of which had their increasingly dense networks of fissures reproduced on the body of local history, as also on that of history as a whole. That this claim is not exaggerated can be demonstrated by reference to the rise of urban history, the outline story of which has deliberately been left until late in the present survey. This form of study and writing is similar to local history (of which it is a complex and advanced form) in that it is an amalgam and not a specialism. It is, on the contrary, a large field of investigation in which specialists – demo-graphic, geographical, social, sociological, political, medical – work on their own account. Its debates have been supervised since 1963–66 by the Urban History Group (UHG),[32] and are well reported in the former *Urban History Yearbook*, but the sheer amorphousness of the field, embracing a multitude of separate, sometimes disparate and often highly specific interests, gives advance warning of what could happen to local and regional history if the pursuers of the latter subjects were not disposed to learn from the character of the impasse reached by their urbanist colleagues. A passingly perceptive comment by a *History Work-shop* editorial not too unfairly summed up the achievements of the UHG by that time, making a major mistake only in asserting that urban history was 'largely a product of British universities' when it was very much an export from the USA:

> its characteristic mode is that of the academic monograph. Urban history is local in scale but curiously distanced from the object of its investigations. Its monographs appear as case studies rather than as exercises in local patriotism – as samples of social structure or illustrations of local growth.[33]

However, the *History Workshop* argument, while correct as far as it then went, and while observant in noting the detachment of academic urbanists from the storms and stresses of town or city life, did not stress the urban historians' failure to demonstrate the nature of urbanizing processes seen as complex wholes.

Several of the 1960s and 1970s pioneers were economic historians interested in economic (and directly related social) influences, and they

accordingly tended to focus very sharply on the role of landownership
in town development. In this case, towns, seaside resorts and suburbs
were made instrumental to an overriding theme which also had potential for social history, and it was this tendency that produced the relatively few outstanding studies attributable to the movement or Group –
the late H.J. Dyos's (1961) own work on Camberwell, Kellett on the
effect of railway landownership in cities, Thompson on Hampstead,
and Cannadine (1980) on Eastbourne and Edgbaston, with a group of
other writers on very specific aspects of individual towns and resorts.[34]
As we shall note, there was an immense literature that was in some way
urban, but it isolated only a few of the main problems in what was a
profoundly complex subject, and by 1975 the Group's chair, Anthony
Sutcliffe, had been obliged to concede that the urbanizing process itself
was neglected.[35] A not too unkind observer of this state of affairs might
have been tempted into the rejoinder that Dyos and his immediate
colleagues had commenced their work at the wrong end of the subject.
Instead of looking for the processes within the growth history of the
small and the smallish town, they had plunged without delay into a
grandiloquent consideration of 'cities'.[36] A biologist might just as well
investigate organs while declining to study cells.[37]

Urban historians were left with fragments instead of cells. There
were, indeed, some enthusiastically conducted local urban studies of the
people's history type, encouraged by History Workshop for approximately five years up to 1980,[38] and promising enough to offer real hope
to local historians living in towns, but it most certainly cannot be said
that urban history as a whole has managed to find more than a widely
variegated area of interest. Meanwhile, the Group's *Urban History
Yearbook* performed a signally valuable service to all historians with
some kind of localized or locational interest by the establishment, in
1974, of the remarkable 'Current Bibliography of Urban History', which
not only showed the range of annually published material with what
purported to be urban implications, but which resoundingly demonstrated the degree of fragmentation which this otherwise thriving activity had achieved.

The 'Current Bibliography' annually included in the region of 1,000
separate articles and books in its list, and three features of this project
are of special interest: first, and not unexpectedly, it swept much local
history into its classifications; second, it threw some real illumination
on the nature of the historical activity within a very large sphere; and,
third, it aspired to be international in scope, ranging over the Anglophone
world and (at first less thoroughly) into Europe. It drew material from a
list of journals running into hundreds, and this pigeon-holing caused by
multiplication of periodicals – as well as of topics – is not one of the

least problems faced by the historian working on particular places. Indeed, the 'Bibliography' inadvertently raised some conundrums in Leicester, its academic home: why should one form of localized history be 'English' and be unwilling consistently to pursue international comparisons, and a later outgrowth be almost religiously internationalist? It appeared that mere localists were having the primitive nature of their study emphasized, and it was typical of the time (the mid-1970s) that debate in local history was unwilling to pose real problems, and was as quiescent as ever. It was also something of a paradox that the urban historians quite evidently did not include city regions within their remit. They could apparently seek an international framework for comparative studies, but not a framework within a city's own hinterland.

The 'Current Bibliography' demonstrated the sheer width and diffuseness of the subject-matter that could be called urban and, in order to control the results of an extraordinary and variegated trawl, it classified the latter into one or other of the following main subject groups: General, Population, Physical Structure, Social Structure, Economic Activity, Communications, Politics and Administration, Shaping the Urban Environment, and Urban Culture and Attitudes to Cities. It will be noticed that these classes were so capacious that, with only slight adaptation, they could have served to cover much of general history as currently pursued, and they could, with other adaptations, have been used to survey many aspects of local and regional history, i.e. any form of history which is in some way localized. The first-named class, General, in fact included much traditional local history that was also about towns, in that the appropriated items dealt with towns in general or with such places seen, however inadequately, in the round. This group, which was like the others in that it was divided into historical periods and stages, included collections of photographs or 'portraits' of towns, and was by far the largest in the bibliography with, in 1975, 417 separate items. Despite niceties of classification, it is not easy to see where most or any of these items could have been brought into a positive general discussion. They were almost wholly descriptive and often antiquarian, and the latter influence often ensures that internal fragmentation is total.

Interestingly, Dyos and his colleagues introduced archaeology into the survey ('Physical and Structural Characteristics of Towns'), giving a lengthy and Hoskins-type time-scale to the bibliography, and a notable period specialization appeared in every main topic. Technology and its approaches, in this case those of building technology and architecture, produced fragments of information from a hemisphere, there was enough on ethnic minorities to satisfy History Workshop or any agency similarly interested, and there was a surprisingly 'thin' section on industry –

indicating not a fault of the bibliographers, but embodying an advance warning of the persisting weakness of economic study at the localized level. Clearly, business history had done little to illuminate the places in which business was carried on. Labour history, too, produced relatively few place-concerned case studies; this point has been made. Urban culture as a subject made a poor showing which, however, improved in the course of time. The general impression is one of a mass of discrete topics, suggesting a multitude of individual acts of appropriation of subject-matter, and a plethora of largely descriptive (or very specialized or analytical) involvements.

Those concerned with the teaching and study of history are, of course, wholly accustomed to this historiographical scene, but let us give a moment's deep consideration to the man or women who is anxious to discover something about his or her own historical and social environment, and then to pose and answer some questions on that environment. Is it any wonder that such a student finds consolation in the pursuit of (let us say) antiquarian data relating to the seventeenth century, or in the more easily assimilable facts of family history? It is also easy to see why those who have some pretensions to local historical scholarship shun the urban history of recent times, and also why so few good general histories of towns have appeared. The field and subject have alike drowned in a welter of fragmented subject-matter – and all this in the absence of determined and even passionate debates which concern the intelligent citizen.

Perhaps, too, this description relates to fields other than that of urban history. However, the challenges to any form of local history remain enormous. Its themes are ostensibly dictated from outside as new and disparate accessions of subject-matter (always plausibly seen as adding to depth of insight) are thrust at the aspirant local historian. This impasse would matter far less if the latter worker had themes and even overriding motivations which could really – to use Finberg's phrase – 'lay under tribute' the products of diversifying specialisms, and there is a desperate need for such themes to pull the fragments together.

There are, unfortunately, other obstacles lying in the way, and we now turn to one of the most serious.

Notes

1. The appearance of West, J. (1983), *Town Records*, as a successor volume to his (1962) highly successful *Village Records*, shows that the rural fixation has not been permanent. This conclusion is strengthened by the marketing of the British Association for Local History publication, Grace,

F. (1992), *The Late Victorian Town*, but also, of course, by many publications on urban history within localities.

2.   Cf. The Report of the Committee to Review Local History (Blake Committee) (1979), 11–21, the section on 'Access to Training'.

3.   This expansion has been brought about by a marked increase in certificates and diplomas in local history, usually by extra-mural departments, in the past ten years. See also data on the growth of East Yorkshire adult classes in local history in Noble M. and Crowther J. (1992), 'Adult Education and the Development of Regional and Local History: East Yorkshire and North Lincolnshire, c. 1929–1985, in P. Swan and D. Foster (eds) *Essays in Regional and Local History*, Hutton Press: Beverley, especially 163–8.

4.   Much use was made of Hoskins (1959) and Finberg's essays (already mentioned), i.e. in training colleges until about 1970, but it is very unlikely that any more controversial sources or ideas were employed, for the simple reason that few of the latter were available.

5.   Garside, P. (1978) 'Local History in Undergraduate History Courses', *Local Historian*, 13, (2), 67, which states correctly that regional history (instead of local) was established in the history courses offered by some universities. The University of Leeds was a pioneer in this respect, largely through the work of G.C.F. Forster.

6.   Pythian-Adams, C. (1987) (revised 1991), *Rethinking Local History*, Department of English Local History Occasional Paper, No. 1, Leicester University Press: Leicester, is the most recent statement of the Leicester position, and represents some significant developments from the positions adopted by Finberg.

7.   Cf. Hudson, P. (ed.), (1989), *Regions and Industries: A Perspective on the Industrial Revolution in Britain*, Cambridge University Press: Cambridge, which has detailed bibliographical references to the regional and economic statements in this sphere.

8.   Knowles, C.H. (*c.* 1983), *Landscape History*, pamphlet, Historical Association.

9.   Finberg, H.P.R. (1962), 'Local History', in H.P.R. Finberg (ed.), *Approaches to History*, Routledge: London, 122.

10.   For the social area, this was identified in the study by *inter alia* Levine D. and Wrightson K. (1979) *Poverty and Piety in an English Village: Terling, 1525–1700*, Academic Press: London, but the idea is traceable to Williams, W.M. (1963), *A West Country Village: Ashworthy*, Routledge: London. For a survey of other literature, stressing that community ties can be in a state of flux and change, see Lewis, G.J. (1979), *Rural Communities,* David and Charles: Newton Abbot, 183–91, and especially p. 188 – the commuter village is one in which local historical societies appear to flourish.

11.   Cf. the quotation on the flysheet of Hoskins, W.G. (1965), *Provincial England: Essays in Social and Economic History*, Macmillan: London and New York.

12.   Tate, W.E. (1946 and successive editions), *The Parish Chest*, Cambridge University Press: Cambridge, is the *locus classicus* for this kind of administrative guidance.

13.   Cf. the telling comments by Widdowson in Marshall, J.D. (1990), (ed.), 'Are British Regions Neglected?', *Journal of Regional and Local Studies*, 10, (2), 36–9.

14. Dymond, D.P. (1974), *Archaeology and History*, Thames and Hudson: London, *passim*.

15. Hoskins, W.G. (1965), 'The Rebuilding of Rural England, 1570–1640', in W.G. Hoskins *Provincial England: Essays in Social and Economic History*, Macmillan: London and New York, 131–48; Machin, R. (1977), 'The Great Rebuilding: An Assessment', *Past and Present*, 77, 33–56.

16. While examples of technological absorption abound, they are seen instructively in *Transactions of the Newcomen Society*, and in *The Industrial Archaeology Review*.

17. Samuel, R. (1976), 'Local History and Oral History', *History Workshop Journal*, (1), Spring, 195.

18. Rix, M. (1953), 'Industrial Archaeology', *Amateur Historian*, 11, (8), marks the beginning of the post-war wave of interest in the subject. It should be noted that the latter had long been represented in the *Transactions of the Newcomen Society*, from the first volume of 1919.

19. Everitt, A.M. , and Tranter M. (1981), *English Local History at Leicester, 1948–1978*, University of Leicester: Leicester, xvi.

20. These topics are taken from the regularly appearing 'List of Publications on the Economic and Social History of Great Britain and Ireland', listed in the *Economic History Review* from 1957 onward. For a statistical survey of all items, see Harte, N.B. (1977), 'Trends in Publication on the Economic and Social History of Great Britain and Ireland, 1925–74' *Economic History Review*, 30, (1), February, 20–41 but especially 34–5.

21. Thirsk, J. (ed.) (1963), 'Work in Progress', *Agricultural History Review*, 11, (1), 103–11.

22. One of the rare instances of this was Pollard, S. and Marshall J.D. (1953), 'The Furness Railway and the Growth of Barrow', *Journal of Transport History*, 1, (1), November, 109–26. Subsequently, it may be noted, the effect of railways on towns and cities became a major theme in urban history (rather than in local), but Dyos was advertising the subject to local historians only a few years later; Dyos, H.J. (1957) 'Counting the Cost of Railways', *Amateur Historian*, 4, (1), Autumn, 191–7. See also *idem* (1955), 'Railways and Housing in Victorian London', *Journal of Transport History*, 2, (1) and (2), May and November.

23. Ashton, T.S. (1958), inaugural statement in *Business History*, (1), December, 2.

24. Samuel, R. (1976), 194.

25. The Cambridge Group, consisting initially of E.A. Wrigley and Peter Laslett, and (somewhat later) Roger Schofield, was formed with the aid of a grant from the Calouste Gulbenkian Foundation in 1963–64. Its first major survey is described in two articles by Wrigley (1964–65), 'Parish Registers and Population History', *Amateur Historian*, (5) and (6), 146–51 and 198–203 respectively. The group also issued newsletters; the first was sent out undated in 1964, the second was dated 13 May 1965 and the third was dated 20 June 1966.

26. This 'vertebrate element' in local history was recognized by several pioneering professionals before the 1960s, and notably by Eversley, D.E.C. (1956–57); see his 'A Survey of Population in an Area of Worcestershire from 1660–1850, on the Basis of Parish Records', *Population Studies*, 10, 253–79. Chambers J.D. (1957), *The Vale of Trent* (*Economic History Review*, supplement No. 3) made much the same point.

27. The relics of this bold intention are to be found in the monumental Wrigley, E.A. and Schofield, R.S. (1981), *Population History of England: 1541–1871*, Edward Arnold: London, *vide* 'List of Parish Characteristics', 39, table 2.3.

28. The relevant literature in this case is Wrigley, E.A. (1966), 'Family Limitation in Pre-industrial England', *Economic History Review*, 19, (1), April; *idem* (1977), 'The Changing Occupational Structure of Colyton over Two Centuries', *Local Population Studies*, 18, 9–21; *idem* (1975), 'Baptism Coverage in Early Nineteenth Century England: the Colyton Area', *Population Studies*, 29, 299–316; Sharpe, P. (1991), 'Literally Spinsters; a New Interpretation of Local Economy and Demography in Colyton in the Seventeenth and Eighteenth Centuries', *Economic History Review*, 44, (1), 46–65.

29. Wrigley and Schofield (1981) do not in reality provide a basis for regional generalizations, although many of their findings can be tested in regional terms, and are thereby valuable. There has recently been a change in emphasis by Cambridge and other scholars however; cf. the studies by McIntosh, M.K. (1986), *Autonomy and Community: The Royal Manor of Havering, 1250–1500*, and its sequel, *idem* (1991), *A Community Transformed*, both Cambridge University Press: Cambridge. These are striking sub-regional surveys given in immense and, at times, over-copious detail.

30. See Samuel (1976).

31. See the interesting judgements on the people's history movement by Savage, M. (1990b), in the section 'People's History and the Local', *Journal of Regional and Local Studies*, 10, (1). Summer, 8–10.

32. The Urban History Group (UHG) grew out of two influences – a growing mass of British postgraduate research on towns, and heavy promotion of urban history in US universities – and its first effective planning meeting, at the Economic History Society Conference of 1963, was undoubtedly stimulated by Briggs, A. (1963), *Victorian Cities*, Odhams: London, and by Dyos, H.J. (1961), *Victorian Suburb: A Study of the Growth of Camberwell*, Leicester University Press: Leicester. Dyos launched an Urban History Newsletter from 1963, and the main launching conference, carefully and comprehensively planned, was at Leicester in September 1966. Thereafter the annual meeting of the UHG was often combined with that of the Economic History Society (it held other conferences elsewhere). It produced the *Urban History Yearbook* from 1974 to 1991.

33. Samuel, R. (1979), 'Urban History and Local History', *History Workshop Journal*, (8), Autumn, iv.

34. Two of the main or seminal studies are included in Note 32; the others are Kellett, J.R. (1969), *The Impact of Railways on Victorian Cities*, Routledge: London; Thompson, F.M.L. (1974), *Hampstead: Building a Borough, 1650–1964*; Routledge: London; Cannadine, D. (1980), *Lords and Landlords: The Aristocracy and the Towns, 1774–1967*, Leicester University Press: Leicester. Other considerable and large-scale urban history has come, in addition, from Sutcliffe, Olsen, Daunton, Chalklin, Sheppard, Walton and a growing list of writers of monographs and theses. The output of large-concept urban history is astonishingly small when measured against the range and number of books and articles in the 'Current Bibliography'. It is likely that many would-be urban historians

are afraid of appearing superficial or disorganized when tackling a town or city in the round; and this, of course, is a consequence of specialization.

35. Sutcliffe, A. (1975), 'The Condition of Urban History in England', *Local Historian*, **11**, (5), February, especially 278.

36. See, for example, Dyos, H.J. and Wolff, M. (eds) (1973), *The Victorian City: Images and Realities*, 2 vols, Routledge: London. Dyos himself seemed to wish to follow the US example in discussion of 'cities' at this period.

37. Regional historians seem to be all too likely to make the same mistakes as the urbanists in neglecting the smaller segments or units; an attempt by the Conference of Regional and Local Historians (1992) to get historians and geographers to discuss 'localities and small regions', including distinctive parts of towns, met with a poor response. At the same time, it should be borne in mind that the latter may have been the result of declining morale in academic life; Dyos built up the UHG using establishment mechanisms and image-promotion, whereas localists and regionalists on the whole remained on the outside.

38. Savage has described this process; see Note 31 above.

The Tyranny of the Discrete:
The Problem of Antiquarianism

Fragmentation is not the only massive problem that bedevils local history. Antiquarianism, by contrast, has been built by tradition into the fabric and study of the subject, and its origins are to be traced into past centuries. It is privately deplored as a fault and an aberration by large numbers of teachers of history, but is little discussed, and is often regarded as a fact of nature and an immovable obstacle which can be circumvented but not reduced.

Dictionary definitions of antiquarianism are singularly unhelpful in their forms of words. It is all very well to be told that the term is defined as 'the profession or pursuit of the antiquarian', who in turn, 'has a taste for, or devotion to antiquities'.[1] That might have been true in Victorian England, just as it is still true of leading members of county learned societies, but it does not come within miles of indicating the significance of the word and concept to the professional historian. It is time that the *Oxford English Dictionary* added to its lists of definitions or variants of meaning, 'an historical heresy', which antiquarianism most decidedly is, or better still, 'an inability to distinguish what features of the past are historically significant; an indiscriminately romantic attitude to the past'.

Not all historians take such an uncompromisingly condemnatory view of antiquarianism. Some see it as an indulgence, a deviation, and even as a form of respectable activity for those whose taste inclines towards careful recording and mining amidst obscure documents. It is, moreover, a gentlemanly activity, especially to the profoundly conservative-minded, and it is further regarded – by those who refuse to make a vulgar fuss about its effects and manifestations – as a thoroughly defensible state or leaning if it results in accurately transcribed documents as published by record societies. It is hard to dissent from this last view; record society publications are frequently a blessing to the student of localized or other forms of history, just as accurately transcribed and printed parish registers are virtually *de rigueur* for the student of local populations or of family reconstitution. The Cambridge Group would have been unable to pursue its projects without them. However, this does not mean that antiquarianism is in itself a Good Thing, but merely that it has side-effects which are sometimes (and perhaps accidentally) useful.

Here it is necessary to distinguish between the preparatory work which all historical investigators must of necessity carry out, in the form of recording, collecting and transcribing, and those activities seen as ends in themselves. The difference between the historical and the antiquarian approaches lies in the way in which the former activities are pursued. As an eminent historian once remarked to the writer, 'the historian is always looking for something', in the sense that he is always putting some agenda in the forefront of his or her mind. The searching will be in evidence even at the most basic stage of assembly of material. Thought, memory, guesswork, planning, exercise of the imagination, the formation of on-the-spot hypotheses, all combine to make the investigation of texts and records alike a fascinating adventure. Students of local history, however, commonly begin their own endeavours in a state of fascination with documents themselves, and present-day modes of instruction, reflected in a seemingly endless flow of publications on local historical sources, seem to ensure that this shall be the case.[2] This output of guides and handbooks is not, however, an index to source-centred instruction alone; it is *au fond* a reflection of the nominally easy availability of documents in an age of record offices and great county and city archive collections. Never have so many historically untrained people come into contact with so many documents. It is this conjunction which gives rise to some unhistorical tendencies discussed here, and which throws into sharp relief the problems created by antiquarianism.

These problems appear on a scale not previously encountered, and are in any case different in kind from those presented by the proto-history and unashamedly gentlemanly antiquarianism of Victorian England. The world of the antiquarian and archaeological societies of that age, as described by P. Levine, was an upper-class world, 'ideologically one with the power structures operating in Victorian Britain'.[3] The gentleman antiquary of that period, concerned with records and genealogy, also had an entrée into the muniment rooms of the wealthy, and it was this individual who gave much of local study its bias – some of which fed through into the early VCH volumes. The latter showed a manifest interest in what were really the instruments or possessions of landowners, in the form of stately homes, castles and churches. We are at this time near to the centenary of the VCH, and the fascinations exerted by such symbols of social and economic dominion, so well displayed in its original pages, have not diminished. At the same time, access to historical information has been, theoretically at least, vastly democratized, that is to say, nine-to-five office employees or some industrial workers still find record offices closed to them but, with this highly important qualification, the searcher has a now threatened but precious access to millions of documents.

This growth of record availability has coincided with a roughly com-
mensurate expansion of tertiary and adult education and, inevitably,
there is a direct connection between the historical (or geographical)
research promoted in academic institutions and the extensive use of
local and national records – and, no less inevitably, with an increasing
output of publications in local and urban history.[4] Given such connections, it is tempting to assume that the democratization of access to
local historical sources has itself played a part in an expansion of local
history as *history*. The reality is altogether more complex and more
worrying. The study of history has expanded because tertiary education
has burgeoned in most of the last 40 years, and that study has seen the
fragmentations described in the last chapter. The popularization of local
history, also an easily verifiable fact, has proceeded in parallel with the
serious or academic study of history, and has been confined in the main
to amateur groups without advanced or formal historical qualifications.
(There have been some important changes in recent years, whereby
graduates in a variety of disciplines have taken diploma or certificate
courses in local history, and recreational groups in the subject have
generally included professional and other middle-class people.) However, as has already been suggested, localized history generally has long
been a complex subject of a kind which offers challenges to the professional and, not surprisingly, amateur groups and individuals have been
unable to set themselves very high standards in their published material.
There are exceptions: fragmented and specialized topics have sometimes
prompted work of diligence and skill but, as we must note, the output
of antiquarian items stays large as its divergence from historical ideas
and discussions widens. Forty years ago, the overflow from this growing stream of amateur publications caused an eminent member of the
Economic History Society (1955) to protest at its overrepresentation in
the lists of articles and books included annually in the *Economic History Review*: 'a miscellany of scribblings has crept in; the antiquarian
and the anecdotal, as well as innumerable snippets from those who can
never resist the temptation of putting pen to paper on however trivial a
subject'.[5]

Moreover, the market for these publications has not only existed and
grown in parallel with that for more serious (i.e. academic) historical
writing, it has certainly kept pace with the latter and has probably far
exceeded it in terms of minor items published. It is, of course, difficult
to make meaningful comparisons. How can one compare a brochure on
a castle or a town hall, or a local newspaper article, with a specialized
book or paper? What is certain is that there is a widespread appetite for
the 'antiquarian and the anecdotal' and, more than this, a popular
response which is in the main completely detached from and uncon-

trolled by exacting critical standards and frameworks of judgement. This detachment, and the reasons for it, are surely worthy of a socio-logical study in themselves, and are almost certainly profoundly related to the limitations and deficiencies of Britain's social and educational systems – and also to folk-attitudes to the past, and to a great and persistent weight of tradition. The subject of primitive antiquarianism, partially embraced in these latter phrases, is touched upon below. Like-wise, the possibility that effective double sets or standards of criteria can obtain in the study and writing of local history is also worthy of the most careful consideration, after all, a valuable mediatory magazine, the *Local Historian* (earlier, *Amateur Historian*) has had to face this problem for many years.[6]

Why do people succumb to 'the temptation of putting pen to paper on however trivial a subject'? The answers are manifold and sometimes seemingly contradictory, and one rather telling rejoinder is that would-be authors have been encouraged to do this by educational missionar-ies, who believe in the formation of adult classes and local societies to promote just such activity. Then, local history consists of 'trivia' to those who work in seemingly more exalted spheres. One cannot envis-age the eminent academics who joined Lord Blake in the Committee to Review Local History (1977–79) taking such a dismissive attitude, for they would see this movement as one of large-scale education and self-education. Moreover, young students in schools have for decades been enabled to look at the past through local instances, just as GCSE examination candidates are now encouraged to use original sources of local historical information, and thereby to become accustomed to looking at the past through what seem to be spectacles of an especially authentic kind. They even use such sources, or copies thereof, to make certain kinds of historical judgement.[7]

The fact remains that in so far as it is possible to generalize about the published output of popular local history in the last 40 to 50 years, its standard is not high in received academic terms, or (far more impor-tantly) in ability to convey sharp, imaginative or exciting insights. In standard and style of approach it has clearly disappointed the propo-nents of people's history, history from the grassroots. In this respect, Samuel's judgements have been significant: 'there (is) a great uniformity about local histories – they call themselves local, but one parish history is more or less interchangeable with another', and elsewhere, posed as a self-justifying question, 'much local history (is) repetitive and inert'.[8] Samuel attributed these failings, in part at least, to the type of docu-ments used by the local researcher: 'one difficulty lies in the nature of the documents, which vary remarkably little from place to place, and which are heavily biased towards local government'.[9] But he made a much more important if less readily obvious point in directing attention to the inherent bias in commonly used local historical documents, in that many of them related to the owners of land or property.[10] Yet, even this questing and lively critic did not comment on the ways in which local history has been taught or otherwise communicated through commonly accessible groups of documents, thereby in some degree stereotyping the resultant history in the manner he describes. Nor did he comment on the attitudes of mind which are fostered through the use of documents by large numbers of people who lack crucial forms of historical training. Above all, in what clearly was and is a most valuable contribution to debate, Samuel did not comment on the hold of antiquarianism on the vast majority of persons who attempt to write local history or to use the documents connected with it.

This was a disappointing omission on the part of a radical historian, for there is undoubtedly an unwillingness to face the implications of the problem on the part of professional teachers and promoters of the subject, who prefer to pretend that the antiquarian problem does not exist, or that they can turn this tendency to good account in teaching – an argument that would be easy enough to accept, if only the subject was ever openly discussed, or if only the educational obstacle and sociological significance alike represented by this aberration was dispassionately analysed. There is, meanwhile, little doubt that in given and suitable cases, students can be rescued from the worst effects of the disease, and sometimes cured altogether, but such remedial work is not done by persons who think that the malady can be extirpated by incantation, or who refuse to recognize it at all.

This unwillingness to confront the problem is frequently visible. The pages of the *Amateur Historian* and the *Local Historian* magazine from 1952 to the present[11] give a very fair impression, both in articles and reviews, of one level of thinking that has lain in the background of local historical teaching and study (mainly but not exclusively in adult education), and the very word 'antiquarianism' barely appears in those pages over a period of 40 years. The present writer introduced it, in the main non-pejoratively, in the course of a debate in the magazine during the years 1963–65[12] and, during the same debate an antiquary, Cox, vigorously defended his standpoint.[13] Yet, not until 1970 did an adult education tutor, Rogers, break ranks and utilize the word and concept in a tone of sharp (and almost certainly well-merited) criticism within a review of a group of local history books. He commented on the style, professional layout and printing of the works concerned, six of which were by amateurs, and on the air of scholarliness that was given to several of these studies by their use of record office sources and local archives. He went on to argue that their work was 'antiquarian nevertheless, for all that it looks so scholarly historical'. Even a professional historian in that group had fallen into this trap by quoting or transcribing sources *in toto*, a common antiquarian habit, and the reviewer made the point, citing Marc Bloch, that 'history is the answer to a series of intelligently posed questions', remarking further that this sample of local 'histories' suffered from being too tied to sources.[14]

This review provoked considerable protest,[15] and one correspondent even commented on the 'unfortunate running battle between professional historians and those they term antiquarians'.[16] There was, over the years, no such 'running battle' in the *Amateur Historian* and *Local Historian*, for the very good reason that seriously controversial articles or reviews rarely appeared, and for the further reason that the magazine concentrated not only on a great variety of topics but, just as consistently, on varied sources for the local historian, rather than on treatment, methodology and material. In this way, it avoided giving more than very occasional offence to the antiquarian-minded, and the few controversial discussions were not maintained or resuscitated. Meanwhile, it should be explained, in fairness to successive editors, that the magazine was tied, after 1961, to two organizations which catered exclusively for amateurs, the Standing Conference for Local History and, from 1981, the British Association for Local History. The editors have had to take account of their often antiquarian readership, while maintaining what was also a very valuable mediatory function and publishing articles by specialist experts in a number of historical fields. In so doing, the magazine yielded inevitably to the fragmentation that was described in the last chapter.

There was, certainly, no consistently pursued debate about the nature and function of local history, and the magazine approached the massive problem of antiquarianism so obliquely that it can have had little direct effect on the intractability of that problem. There was just enough debate to give an impression of deafening silence during, let us say, 36 of the magazine's 40 plus years of existence. The purpose of this comment, however, is not to dwell on the approaches of those who ran the journal, but rather to emphasize the powerful and negative effect of the popular market for local history. (The provision of academically moderated training courses for leisure-time students has given the educational side of local history an appreciable step forward, remembering always that the types of problems discussed here must, like the real nature of regional history, be given an examination that is full and fair.)

Antiquarianism, as it now appears, is a social and a general educational phenomenon, and more is said on that subject below. The educational side of the burgeoning local history movement in Britain has nevertheless created a serious, if unrecognized, problem for itself by document-centred teaching, a fashion which originally stimulated and grew out of public demand at one and the same time. This approach and fashion had deep roots in the adult education movement, and was being practised by a noted pioneer, the late F.W. Brooks of Hull and Leeds, in the 1930s.[17] However, the post-war boom in the subject meant that there was a shortage of experienced part-time adult class tutors in local history, and classes were often taken by schoolteachers, librarians and archivists with a personal interest in localities – and these exponents quickly found that copies of documents held in record offices and reference libraries[18] were rivetingly interesting to members of classes, who responded to what they felt was a direct link with the local past. This movement also created a public for the highly successful primers by Hoskins, Celoria and Pugh.

The lecturers or tutors, meanwhile, often had limited professional training in history, and were certainly not immune to antiquarian influences. Even where the tutor had the status of a professional historian, he or she was working in a field that enjoyed relatively little esteem in academic terms. Indeed, the tutor might have acquired a little glory from learned papers or a book or two on the locality, but in the library reference room in which his or her classes took place were the handsomely bound volumes of the county learned society, bearing witness to the utter and lasting solidity of antiquarian values. Who was this person to question the permanence, scholarliness and worth of what lay spread out in scores of elegantly printed (and often regrettably unimaginative) articles? It is now fairly clear that many such instructors pursued the policy of the estimable *Local Historian* in failing to confront the antiquarian problem, for such a confrontation would have been daunting as well as difficult. Many more lacked the inclination or the equipment to do so.

Now, let us look at the doubtless sociable and thriving class from the standpoint of the student. The latter was (and still is) immediately offered a privilege that is denied to most university history students in the greater parts of their courses, in that he or she, the student, is excitingly enough given a close view of the actual sources of historical information almost from the first meeting. It is here that the historically qualified reader must transfer himself or herself into the mind of the tyro and to begin by recalling the scent of his or her first historical document, and its footprint-like aura as it seemed to carry messages from an inscrutable past. It is easy to overlook its fragile wonder, and its import, however trivial, has a uniqueness and incontrovertibility about it which cannot be denied. The student's highly personal view of the past, seen through a tiny chink in the generally mysterious, appeals to a mixture of voyeurism and curiosity. Historians who use a trained imagination in unravelling past events must also remember that the untrained imagination has its charms. After all, what can be more absorbing than an inner vision of the man who wrote the words on the parchment, his characters conveying the sense of his muscular effort as he formed the letters, and his words and style themselves carrying the imprint of a human personality over the centuries? Then, the scribe was not just *any* man; he was a man who lived *in this place*. Traces of the past, seen in this way, are beguiling in the extreme, and many users of records never lose this pristine sense of fascination.

It is this mixture of fascination and absorption that serves to explain the repeated support for courses in which local history has been approached through records. The student is enabled to commune with the past in his or her own way, without a spiritual intermediary to order him or her in one direction or another. Many students discover that they need a framework of methodology and discipline, and fair numbers are willing to absorb what is at least a modicum of these requirements, just as other students learn to look up such general historical information as they require. The approach, however, is essentially narrow, individualistic and restricted in view, and it acquires its value to the student from the overriding fact of the past itself, reflected in the individual document seen as a discrete object. Many students, again, are encouraged to learn to generalize (even at the local level) by their tutors, but generalization on such a narrow front can seem dull – and can actually divert the student from the real origin of his or her pleasure. The source or document is manageable, and it has its own reality. History, on the other hand, cannot take shape without some kind of generalization. The instructor must therefore face a series of very real likelihoods:

1. The student, having given the source precedence in his or her interests and affections, will continue to do so. His or her world will therefore become source-centred and, almost inevitably, antiquarian.
2. If the student remains absorbed in original sources, he or she will be content to reproduce information from those sources, which he or she will regard as having special historical validity. In other words, the information itself will become a substitute for history; the discrete fact itself becomes pseudo-history.
3. In any case, a student without some broader historical education will in most cases not know how to develop a historical argument based on sources as evidence. Only in recent decades has the more general historical education of (say) adult class groups in local history been seriously regarded, and it is often believed that stu-

dents educate themselves historically through specific local studies. Historical self-education of a genuine and comprehensive kind is in fact rarer than may appear, and is not necessarily transferable from narrow exercises.

4. Students in the classes mentioned are likely to develop the notion that crucial or important historical information comes from manuscript sources only. This leaves them unable to appreciate an argument which uses a variety of different sources to provide evidence.

5. They are also prone to develop a prejudice to the effect that facts are more important than arguments, and that the verification of facts represents almost the sum total of local historical activity. The editors of the *Local Historian* have themselves had to face this supremacy-of-facts mentality[19] which, incidentally, is inadvertently encouraged by most popular guides and textbooks on local history. The writer has yet to encounter one of the latter which explains to the reader that historical 'facts 'are man-made and far from immutable, and – marvel of marvels should the proposition appear – that a hunger for the purely factual has socio-political as well as psychological implications, as suggesting a desire for security, stability and an unchanging mental or political state.

Some of these attitudes and sentiments can, over a long period, be encased in a relative sophistication, especially in the milieu of the regional learned society or the received gentlemanly form of antiquarianism. The exponent will display an attitude of pronounced humility towards historians and the past. He or she will not aspire even to pass a judgement on a given problem or controversy, and his or her interest is in producing factual information which may, or may not, throw light on some small aspect of the subject, it being implied in the politest possible manner that much of the noise made by historians is vain and even arrogant. While this apparent smugness may enrage or provoke the teacher of history who comes into contact with it, there is sometimes another emotional root beneath it: the practitioner derives considerable satisfaction from being able to control and organize documentary information, and may sometimes deploy very real convergent skills in interpreting the contents of manuscripts. We are, in such cases, reminded that there are different forms of antiquarianism, some of which can be genuinely supportive of history, and others of which may just conceivably turn out to be so. The fact remains that great resources of printing and publication are utilized to record information of dubious or uncertain application, in an age when our unfortunate schools are often perennially short of books and equipment. With better history teaching there would probably be less of an antiquarian problem.

Before examining the matter of historical education – and the preva-lence of antiquarianism among supposedly educated people in the world at large leaves no room for complacency – it will be well to look more closely at the forms taken by the latter. It should be established immedi-ately that a blanket dismissal of the malady, as performed by the late Sir Geoffrey Elton (who has seen it as something which finds a natural and harmless home in 'parish history, local archaeology, genealogy, lawyer's history of the law'),[20] is merely passing the implicit educational problem to others. We can leave aside the possibility that Sir Geoffrey's col-leagues among the fraternity of political historians have had in reality far less excuse for their own antiquarian deviations than has any parish amateur,[21] and instead concentrate on the different manifestations of this attitude of mind.

First, then, we have what is essentially a naïve and vaguely curious attitude that is experienced by many millions of citizens when they visit a museum or great house. In so far as individuals wonder about the past, and ask mental questions about it, then this state of mind, which we shall call *primitive antiquarianism*, is a potentially valuable one. Unfortunately, most adult persons do not pass beyond it and, much worse, this mental set or state is easily exploited by groups and institu-tions which treat the citizen as a paying consumer, and which sell packaged versions of what purports to be history. There is a school of thought which says 'better this than no history at all', but this defence soon loses conviction when its proponents are asked to consider the possibility that such packaged history sooner or later destroys curiosity. It provides little or no foundation for basic building or enlargement and, of course, no system of critical thought is ordinarily connected with it. What is much more worrying, this form of approach to the individual reaches him or her most commonly through discrete objects or constructions. Instead of finding fascination in a document, like the beginner in a local history class, the client or consumer looks at a building, an implement or a machine, and is told how to respond to it.

This involvement with the discrete, with the individual object, is greatly buttressed by the spectacular increase in museums and museum displays in the past 20 years, but also by some aspects of archaeology as pursued at the local level. Since the last may be seen as a contentious point, then it will be well to acknowledge immediately that archaeology seen as a whole is a system of historical thought, the raw material and evidence for which often takes the form of discrete objects examined locally – but which may have little significance for the history of a locality as such. In any case, archaeology and antiquarianism have close emotional and psychological as well as procedural connections, and have joint roots extending into past centuries. Many learned societies combine the two forms of study, which may appear either in their constitutions or in their titles (like the Cumberland and Westmorland Antiquarian and Archaeological Society). However, it must also be conceded that the broader British public knows little of the activities of these bodies. On the other hand, the broader public does visit museums and, sometimes, archaeological sites in its millions. What is more, those museums are often held to have an educational function, in that children are shown objects from the past that are felt to give reality to the past. Objects may seem to acquire an even greater reality if displays are 'hands on', and the schoolchild is permitted to handle them. This process may in turn be held to provide support (or ballast) for local history and other teaching, undertaken in connection with the National Curriculum, and an article taken almost at random from the journal *Teaching History* puts its case in these words:

> objects ... lead to a deeper understanding of the people who made and used them. Direct contact between the child and the object can provide a wonderful stimulus in the evaluation and interpretation of historical evidence. It is difficult to over-estimate the help that museum objects can provide for pupils in the study of all aspects of local history.[22]

Several problems arise here. First, the proponents of this type of argument seem to overlook the possibility that the teacher is in this instance laying the foundation not of an historical education, but merely of a strengthened primitive antiquarianism, leading to the swelling of future numbers of customers for Heritage sales points. Next, the object may, in this process, be fundamentally a mnemonic, like a weight holding some simple historical evocation or explanation in place. The child is likely to be surrounded by a mass of 'mnemonics', many of them confusing and lacking context or ultimate significance – and what happens to the pupil can provide something of an analogy regarding the adult visitor to the same museum, who may relate many individual items or objects to his or her own more mature experience, but who cannot (understandably) use the explanatory legends to fit this experience into a much wider context. He or she is continually confronted by the specific, and the student's chances of understanding the general may be made progressively more remote.

It is here that one must make the most crucial point of this entire argument, one that is implicit in the case put by this short book: local history, like any other kind of history, is meaningless without coherent, immediate, imaginative and above all *telling* context, and it is precisely this which is lacking in many museum collections and their presentations, and in Heritage displays. They are inert and are often incapable of stimulating curiosity beyond the casual, although they can also be notably useful to a person (or consumer) who is already informed and who is looking for further information about manners, skills or technologies. This agreeable consolation, unfortunately, does not round off our list of troubles. The techniques of presentation of museum displays have waxed on the foundation of their own visitor appeal, and the past is re-created for the consumer in the form of elaborately furnished period rooms, groups of figures, workmen in workshops, battlefield scenes and the like, all in such ways that the viewer has no room left for his imagination to work. The latter is injected with what Umberto Eco has called hyper-reality, which makes the past seem more real than a shifting and uncertain present.[23] But the trip into past 'reality' is an encapsulated trip, detached from wider perceptions, and is part of a more sophisticated but educationally blind antiquarianism, still largely primitive. The teacher who salutes it, the class tutor who welcomes it, are the victims of self-delusion; the visual aid has taken over the subject itself. This process is implied resoundingly in the phrase landscape history. There is no history in the landscape unless there are people evidently interacting within it. A record of traces is not history.

As will be all too evident, the foundations of primitive antiquarianism are built into the relevant aspects of our formal and informal systems of education. The undiscriminating use of documents in school, the exploitation of casual interest and nostalgia by the media (local newspapers, with their 'factual' and rubbernecking articles on local historical themes, visits to supposedly significant historical sites as presented in TV or local radio), the stress on archives (rather than on historical interpretation) which is common even in responsible public discussions, the underpinning of what are really antiquarian attitudes by popular and industrial archaeology movements, all of these make collectively a powerful anti-historical force – so powerful that it seems astonishing that historians remain untroubled by it. The latter seem to console themselves that because there is evidently an interest in 'the past', all is well. Pieces of this past can be marketed, and even examined: it is this mentality that sees much local history as a homogeneous marketable commodity and not as one or other aspect of primitive antiquarianism.

The next variant of antiquarianism can be termed *formalized*. This is the scholarly and gentlemanly form, and its context or framework is that of the county or city learned society, but also that of the Society of Antiquaries of London, the Monumental Brass Society, The Royal Commission on Ancient and Historical Monuments, the Society for Mediaeval Archaeology, the Society for Post-Mediaeval Archaeology, and a constellation of groups concerned with the recording, conservation and preservation of buildings, notably English Heritage itself. The Heraldry

Society and the Institute of Heraldic and Genealogical Studies most certainly belong spiritually to this group. Record societies have been omitted deliberately from this list because they relate more closely to the following sub-class, the *proto-historical* form of antiquarianism. Meanwhile, it is this formidable assemblage of highly ordered and convergent learning that gives respectability and weight to formalized antiquarianism, connecting itself through a multiplicity of unconscious and unremarked links to strong conservative elements in the historical establishment. One feels that it is there that Sir Geoffrey Elton should have directed his fire.[24]

The speciality of this large and varied group of recorders and scholars is not so much the discrete object, but the site, instance or example either related to a formalized class or group (about which a great deal is known already), or detached from any stated context old or new. There are signs that the subject-matter accumulated by these groups is currently open to exploitation by social or anthropological historians, but that was not intended by the scholars themselves. Their cast-iron respectability gives continual warrant and apparent spiritual support to the most unimaginative compilers in the counties and localities, and it appreciably underpins the work of the county societies.

A word should be said about the latter. Their activities have been increasingly influenced during the past generation or two by incursions of academic historians, who are thereby apt to think that formalized antiquarianism is no longer a problem at the regional level. Those who hold such a view should permit themselves to browse through the thousands of county learned society volumes in the Library of the Institute of Historical Research or other great academic collections. These may suggest that the professional historians' influence is nothing like as great as the latter are apt to imagine. The function of the historian in such a case is merely that of making the regional transactions academically acceptable. The articles in the societies' volumes, for their part, exalt accuracy and formal learning, but do little for imaginative regional or local study. Popular and community local history gets little aid and stimulus from such sources, and there is a yawning social, and psychological, divide between the formal antiquarianism of the one and the would-be grass roots history of the other.

Finally, there is another and distinguishably useful form of antiquarianism, the proto-historical kind. Examples of this genre have been given at the commencement of the present chapter. However, there are two variants even of this sub-class, namely printed works that are useful by accident (such as the parish register transcripts used with great effect by the Cambridge Group), and those which are useful because they are in reality part of some historical debate, strategy or plan. The formal antiquaries will often claim that their work falls into this category, but the remedy, where disputation arises, lies firmly in their hands; they should have the courtesy to state, in book or article, the relevance of their work to wider discussions, and should not pretend that such guidance implies a lapse of good manners. In general, record transcripts are proto-historical because, however antiquarian the leanings of the transcriber, the final product will almost certainly have helpful historical applications. Antiquarian obtuseness, however, will sometimes cause the editorial committees of record societies to be insensitive to popular demand or obvious application, but it is expediency that will occasionally cause them to pick and edit a set of manuscripts for no better reason than they have to hand an editor who can keep the flow of publications in being.

Where does this leave us? Historians who have swallowed the camel of antiquarianism for a lifetime, by pretending that it is pleasantly recreational and therefore contributory to the health and happiness of mankind, are hardly likely to kindle – save in a negative sense – at the considerations here set out. The man or woman who cares about the history of his or her own locality or native territory may react differently. That person may resent the idea that the residents of a community should be left, as a consequence of a conscious policy on the part of informed people, without the understanding of the past that serious history strives to reach and to set forth, and he or she may find the idea of double standards in local history to be a repugnant one, leading to the idea of first- or second-class citizens, with purposeful history as the privilege of the one and primitive antiquarian bread and circuses as the portion of the second. The antiquarian debate concerns educational and intellectual standards and integrity at their most fundamental. In an age when the academic world has had its nose well rubbed in consumerism, and when it is forced to think in terms of the consumer appeal of courses, these crucial concerns are all too easily neglected.

What can be done in the practical sphere? First, serious historians should cease to regard localized history as a mere source of data, that is, as instrumental, and should recognize that it represents an enormous challenge in an age of specialist fragmentation. Secondly, they should think of involving citizens in those challenges; after all, their own locality and forbears are part of the story. Thirdly, all those who are involved in teaching and investigating local history should strive to set it into context, supra-local, regional and national. This is what has been conspicuously lacking in every aspect of the popularly pursued subject in the post-war years. It has been assumed that individuals or groups can write a history of their locality without reference to the town or village next door. In this respect, H.P.R. Finberg's warning about the dangers of 'national history localized',[25] the product of an attempt to give Leicester local history an academic identity, was almost certainly mischievous. To commence with the likely influence of the nation (or region) on a locality is a sensible beginning; the peculiarities can be discovered as the local contexts are understood.

One final thought may be worthy of consideration. Techniques of drawing the innumerable victims of primitive antiquarianism into the real excitements and insights of history are worthy of conscious and sustained endeavour. Nor need there be overmuch despair at the magnitude of the task; the important thing is to begin the campaign. In a situation whereby there is a tyranny not only of the discrete, but of objects from the past in general, the mere act of discussion of the context and relevance of a single object destroys at a stroke, temporarily, the immediately antiquarian. No teacher or tutor should neglect this precautionary discussion. It may then be possible to make some good and effective history from the narrow obsessions of the conservation movement, which themselves threaten to usurp history.[26] Too few teachers of local history will readily set up a firm but polite challenge to the insidious and anti-historical influence of the latter, for fear of alienating potential leisure-time students – but this does not have to happen. Meanwhile, what serious teacher can undermine the validity of his or her own subject?

Notes

1. *Oxford English Dictionary* (1989), vol. 1, 2nd edn, 531. This simply repeats the formulation of the earlier edition of 1933!
2. There are astonishingly few books on local historical themes or methodology; the successive editions of Laslett (1965), *The World We Have Lost*, Methuen: London, or the work of Macfarlane (1977a), *Reconstructing Historical Communities*, Cambridge University Press: Cambridge, at least suggest what is missing. Hey, D. (1987), *Family History and Local History in England*, Longman: London, is an enthusiastic and imaginative popularization which fills some of the gaps, and which is willing to look the recent world in the eye. Horn, P. (1976), *Labouring Life in the Victorian Countryside*, Gilland Macmillan: Dublin and London, is one of a number of similar works which help the local historian to find a theme. By contrast, there is a long list of books on sources and archives, of which the following make a representative sample: Emmison, F.G. (1978), *Introduction to Archives*, Phillimore: Chichester; Tate, W.E. (1946 and later editions to 1983), *The Parish Chest*, Cambridge University Press: Cambridge; Stephens, W.B. (1973) *Sources for English Local History*, Manchester University Press: Manchester; Iredale, D. (1973), *Enjoying Archives*, David and Charles: Newton Abbot; West, J. (1962, 1982), *Village Records*, Macmillan: London; West, J. (1983), *Town Records*, Phillimore:

Chichester; Stuart, D. (1992), *Manorial Records*, Phillimore: Chichester; Alcock, N.W. (1986), *Old Title Deeds*; Oliver, G. (1989), *Photographs and Local History*; Chapman, C. (1991), *English Education Records*; Thoyts, E.E. (1980), *How to Decipher and Study Old Documents*, Elliot Stock: London; Porter, S. (1990), *Sources for Local Historians*; Hindle, P. (1988), *Maps for Local History*; Riden, P. (1987), *Record Sources for Local History*, Batsford: London. This list does not take account of guides and bibliographies issued by county record offices, or of instruction books on family history or the making of transcripts from the Latin – and it should be noted that most of these books are recently in print. This is a case of the market following a demand for the raw material of local history but rarely for history itself, and of the dominance of the source-centred approach.

3. Levine, P. (1986), *The Amateur and the Professional*, Cambridge University Press: Cambridge, 12–14.

4. See Note 5 below; Harte demonstrates trends in, for example, local history publishing in the article cited.

5. Coleman, D.C. (quoted with express permission to the author) in Harte, N.B. (1977), 'Trends in Publications on the Economic and Social History of Great Britain and Ireland, 1925–74', in *Economic History Review*, 30, (1), February, 29. However, the Council of the Economic History Society (1959) was anxious that the 'junk' should be retained, apparently by virtue of the quarry-values attached to local history.

6. The editor (1955) of the *Amateur Historian*, 2, (5), April–May, 129, saw a difference between 'works of general historical significance and local histories'. But it was necessary to consider what might happen if one of the latter publications *did* (like Levine and Wrightson's more recent work) turn out to be of 'general historical significance'. The editor clearly felt himself to be under real pressure to erect a set of easier alternative standards to benefit the untrained amateur. The problem here is to assess where such double standards are likely to lead.

7. Examples of such teaching approaches appear in three articles in the *Amateur Historian* (1965), 6, (7), Spring, 218–26. Also, see James, T. (1987) 'Using Local History in the GCSE: A Practical Exercise on the Leawood Canal', *Local History*, (15), 12–14; Rea, T. (1988), 'A Local Study at Tutbury Hill', *Local History*, (16), January, 14–16. There is now a large literature in this field.

8. Report of Oral History Society Conference (issued by and quoted with permission of the Society) at London School of Economics, 2 November 1974; Samuel, R. (1976), 'Local History and Oral History', *History Workshop Journal*, (1), Spring, 193.

9. Samuel, (1976).

10. Samuel, (1976), 194.

11. The *Amateur Historian* was acquired by the Standing Conference for Local History in 1961, and changed its name to the *Local Historian* in 1968. The editor between 1955 and 1975 was L.M. Munby, a well-known adult education tutor in Herts. and elsewhere. See Munby, L.M. (1992), 'Reflections on Times Past', *Local Historian*, 22, (1), February, 8–13.

12. Marshall, J.D. (1963), 'The Use of Local History: Some Comments', *Amateur Historian*, 6, (1), Autumn, 11–13.

13. Cox, D. (1965), 'Antiquarianism and Local History', *Amateur Historian*, 6, (8), Summer, 160–1.
14. Rogers, A. (1970), Review Section, *Local Historian*, 9, (3), 141–5.
15. Munby, L.M. (1977), 'Reminiscences and Reflections of an Ex-Editor', *Local Historian*, 12, (7), 333.
16. Ibid.
17. Brooks, F.W. (1973) 'Local History, 1930–48', *Local Historian*, 10, (8), 386. This noted tutor was a medievalist who made much use of antiquarian sites, castles, abbeys and so forth and, given the problems raised in the present discussion, it has remained unclear how far such campaigning relied for its impact on antiquarian sentiment on the part of students, and how far it modified their responses. Brooks was a deeply enthusiastic teacher with much success in expanding student interest attributable to his work, but his valedictory article (above) shows a worrying if understandable lack of self-doubt.
18. It should not be forgotten that local library reference collections burgeoned during the same years; Foster, J. and Sheppard, J. (1982), *British Archives: A Guide to Archive Resources in the United Kingdom*, Macmillan: London, xxiv.
19. For example, Munby (1977), 333: 'Please give us reliable facts.'
20. Elton, G.R. (1969), *The Practice of History*, Fontana: London, 152.
21. Elton, (1969), 152–4.
22. Barwell, J. (1990), 'Museums and the National Curriculum', *Teaching History*, October, 28.
23. Eco, U. (1987), *Travels in Hyper-Reality*, Picador: London, 1-58.
24. Elton, G.R. (1969), 152–4.
25. Finberg, H.P.R. (1962), 'Local History', in H.P.R. Finberg (ed.) *Approaches to History*, Routledge: London, 116, for this scholar's last explicit statement of the idea.
26. Cf. Lowenthal, D. and Binney, M. (1981), *Our Past Before Us: Why Do We Save It?*, Temple Smith: London, which is in the main a collection of sensible but rather limited essays in favour of conservation at a variety of levels. The real historical questions are not addressed.

CHAPTER FOUR

The Community Obsession in English Local History

After all that has been said so far, the Hoskins and Finberg statement of the main theme of English local history – 'the Origin, Growth, Decline and Fall of a Local Community'[1] – which has held sway for a generation or more, may be regarded as somewhat *passé*. Here, however, we must exercise care. Such an unqualified formulation no longer represents the explicit Leicester position,[2] but the broad idea of the local community has taken firm hold, and it surfaces in relatively recent general guides to local history.[3] An examination of these representative guides shows that much has changed in the course of 40 years: the survey by Tiller (1992), *English Local History: An Introduction*, indicates that there has been a real attempt, on the part of a resourceful teacher, to absorb the fragmentation so far described, and to provide new insights into 'the local community' with the aid of more and more methodological tools. But the impact of such fragmentation may still be a powerful one, with an all too likely psychological effect on the student, the result of which can easily be general disorientation alongside over-concentration on given topics. This, in turn, has bearing on the community-type long-sweep narrative associated with the Leicester school. The survey by Lewis (1989), *Particular Places*, also demonstrates the influence of some important developments in recent decades, including the rise of family as well as urban history and, in particular, illustrates the influence of regional history. However, it is worth noticing that this author also places special emphasis on the local 'community' – in its medieval form 'a community of worshippers' – one which was held together by economic and social bonds during much of its history.[4] As a social entity, the latter might, in Lewis's view, last through the nineteenth and into the twentieth century.[5]

Lewis's view of the local historical scene is a much wider one than has been common, but he does not manage incidentally to show how the fragmenting parts fit together and, again, the student of 'particular places' will be rendered uncertain by the options presented to him. Part of this widening of view was made possible by the growing popularity of regional history in academic institutions in the 1960s and later, and this institutionalization of a more generalized form of the local variety received its expression in the three journals *Northern History* (1966),

Midland History (1971), and *Southern History* (1981), each of which remains influential in its sphere, and each of which has been of interest to many scores of academics and students working at a level above the specifically rural and local – commonly at that of urban and county history. The developments described by Lewis, which have been partially reflected in the work of professional historians with localized interests, rest only incidentally on any position taken by the Leicester scholars, whose work has understandably continued to stress the study of local communities. In so doing, the Leicester historians have underpinned such relatively specific theoretical assumptions as have appeared important to students of this form of history.

These theoretical considerations are nevertheless central to the subject. Discussion concerning them has developed slowly, fitfully and unevenly (that is, most frequently at Leicester), because the conditions for debate have hardly been favourable during the last 40 years. We have to conclude that those conditions have been lacking despite a number of attempts to introduce debate,[6] and it is clear that the time is now overdue for a much more critical examination of the problems of present-day local history. One can only speculate on the reasons for this apparent intellectual inertia, but it seems extremely likely that prominent among them is the sheer convenience of the subject for the achievement of goals divergent from the enlargement and deepening of local history for its own sake. The Leicester scholars have been to the fore in advocating the latter aim. It may be, too, that in the words of the philosopher of history W.H. Walsh, 'a subject develops a philosophy only when it is a matter of more or less acute controversy'.[7] Quite simply, there has been, to many, no discernible gain in seemingly fruitless debate within a field which has resembled a growth industry more than an academic subject – and which has often been, as far as a wider world is concerned, antiquarian or deeply empiricist.

Notwithstanding this tendency to erudite recital, the seeds of controversy have always lain within the local historical soil of the last four decades. It is astonishing that a number of contentions by Finberg, relating to 'the local community', have gone almost unchallenged during that period, just as it now seems scarcely less puzzling that some kind of critical groundswell was not set going by a number of relevant interventions in the 1950s and 1960s.[8] However, Finberg's case clearly seemed to be persuasive to large numbers of intelligent readers and enthusiastic students, and it is worthwhile rehearsing some of its main elements.

For example, Finberg saw the local community as 'a social entity',[9] one which was evidently to be determined empirically, and this idea, then (1962) not very closely defined or developed, fitted very comfortably into the document-centred activity and pursuit of local history that was encouraged in training college and adult class alike. The social entity, he argued, had 'a perfectly good claim to be studied for its own sake', and its pursuit and identification was not simply a part of the subject-matter of national history. The local community, meanwhile, was 'a closely integrated social formation which (had) been an ever-present, not to say obsessive, reality for many thousands of people through the centuries'.[10] (It is not clear what the 'thousands' actually signified.)

It is hard not to feel some sympathy for Finberg's case thus far, and it is true that many people cherish close ties to their place of origin and nurture, and the feeling for locality is probably as strong as affection for that abstract entity known as the nation, if not much stronger. (Patriotism, it may be assumed, is a blend of both of these attachments.) However, it becomes clear that Finberg is describing something more than a group of people with similar ties of attachment to a given place. He is discussing a local society, or social entity, which shares similar goals, and which can act collectively in a number of situations. Nor is he describing villages or parishes only; he asserts that 'even a shire could feel and act as a self-conscious unit', citing a petition of 'the community of the whole county' of Kent in 1313.[11] It is perhaps unfortunate that this distantly historical use of a word like 'community' can be elided into one with a great range of modern sociological connotations and resonances. Taking his case further, Finberg also saw the local community, that of the village in this case, as bound together by institutions (or, more properly, by the ongoing sentiments, ideas and practices within those institutions) and, it would seem, by further ties of deference to a lord of the manor – 'the fealty to the lord of the manor (which) provided the community with a recognised head', the lord providing in turn 'a court that served as the local organ of justice and administration'.[12] The ties, in other words, were both horizontal and vertical. It is also worth noticing that Finberg invoked justice and administration, but did not mention power or coercion.

It becomes clear that Finberg was describing a social entity which was, on the whole, based on harmony of belief and opinion, and even on a form of crude or basic democracy. He made an assumption concerning the Tudor and Stuart 'unity of belief and worship that found its rallying point in the parish church', and further concerned 'the young of all ranks (who) continued to learn their letters at the local grammar school'.[13] The first of these assumptions, relating to the binding effect of religion, appears in Lewis's *Particular Places*, cited above, and has also found detailed expression in *Contrasting Communities* by Spufford (1974), while the implied role of the grammar school is simply misleading; the open or charitable activity of that institution was seated on a great mass of non-literate culture. The 'unity of belief and worship' is belied by every writer on religious dissent, and by many striking and ironic references in consistory court records.[14] It seems that in invoking an idealized rural or village community, Finberg was telling students of local history what to look for, when he should have been telling them what to question and to test.

Finberg was advocating that his researcher saw the local community in an idealized, organic sense, and as one which worked as a self-sustaining and self-reproducing whole religiously, educationally, and agriculturally or economically. The same persuasive message surfaces in *Particular Places* nearly a generation later: 'In pre-industrial England, the different types of communal bonds ... religious, civil and economic – reinforced one another to a remarkable degree'.[15] It is too easy to make suppositions about neighbourly linkages, the effects of the multiple contacts in a parish congregation, and the permanent consequences of relying upon neighbours with parish or manorial responsibilities. We do not really know how often people were in contact, and still less do we know what their real sentiments were. Insights into the behaviour of local societies as a whole are chronologically scattered, and are less easy of achievement than propagandists for local history like to suggest.

Meanwhile, we should remember again that Hoskins and Finberg saw the local community as having a biological life-line over time, embodying 'Origin, Growth, Decline and Fall' (or final disintegration), and it is here germane to add that this view of a biological, organic community was widespread at that period, and was comprehensively reflected in the work of the US sociologist Hawley (1950), who developed the *ecological* view of the local community. This stressed the physical and environmental characteristics of the community area, and it saw men and women as responding individually and collectively to the habitat in which they lived, to such an extent that human behaviour reflected the latter's main general features.[16] There is a parallelism between the world of Hoskins's Midland peasants and this latter view, and even more in the developing Leicester concept of landscape as both moulding and reflecting history. Although this last idea has seemed to appeal handsomely to common sense, it imported deterministic (and therefore at times misleading) assumptions into discussion of environments, which have in turn influenced a generation of local historians. The richness of human interactions, and the pervasiveness of cultures, are too often overlooked.

The biological or growth-disintegration metaphor does not in any case lay bare the roots of historical change in a 'community', and it smuggles in value judgements about 'fullness of (the community's) life and vigour' or even 'perfection' of development – and equally about the dire impact of 'the world of megapolis or what the town planner calls conurbations'. It may indeed be true that some agrarian or rural centres, once the railways had arrived, 'became backwaters and sank into a death-like trance'.[17] The implied value judgement suggests that a community reaches an ideal state and then departs from it over time. In other words, the Leicester approach was one of historical and philosophical idealism, which concentrated on the rural village or market centre, and which exalted the ways of life there encountered in a largely pre-industrial period.

Yet, it was at the point of transmutation from rural to industrial that the really sharp questions about the nature of communities were likely to be asked and, perhaps understandably, the Leicester scholars in the main kept away from this putative battleground. No doubt they felt that their work covered a huge swathe of pre-industrial history, and that they had no warrant to be pursuing a contentious last chapter. They gained much in the way of respectability and easy acceptance – and there was more. As we may now deduce, their 'community' in fact 'threatened nobody – particularly as it was becoming defunct!'[18] However, it is the argument here that the real questions were avoided not merely because of the particular form of historical idealism adopted by the Leicester scholars, but also because the latter were uninterested – as many academics were at that time uninterested – in the educational as well as the philosophical implications of local historical study. It was one thing to interest large numbers of amateur or part-time students in an idealized local community that could only be easily examined through the adoption of Leicester assumptions about its nature, but it was quite another to divert their interests from the world in which they were actually living, a world that many students recognized and partly understood. Good teaching should have rested on human experience within living communities.

It was in this respect that the absence of debate was particularly reprehensible, because sustained critical discussion would almost certainly have revealed serious local historical lacunae, like the non-appearance of good nineteenth- or twentieth-century local studies, save those produced by sociologists like Margaret Stacey or W.M. Williams. As Parker has justly pointed out, Hoskins's historical world did fall into a degree of escapism notwithstanding his angry rebuttal,[19] and one might add to this that Finberg, perhaps to Hoskins's private discomfiture, assumed a highly conservative and deferential local society, some of the features of which have already been noted. In short, one cannot imagine that this view of local history would have offended leisured ladies in county local history committees (even though the latter are often much more independent-minded, given a chance, than some would expect).

Notwithstanding the educationally uncertain gains reaped by the original successes of the Leicester school, the latter did, thanks to the undoubted originality of some of its best students, produce at least two works which moved the community debate forward, and which both added to and broadened its content in a largely practical sense. The studies by Spufford (1974), *Contrasting Communities*, and by Hey (1974), *Myddle under the Tudors and Stuarts*, both appeared rather too early to benefit from any debates promoted by the Social History Society, formed soon afterwards, or by History Workshop and, of the two studies, Margaret Spufford's work was the more truly original and genuinely important. She made the obvious and basic point that historical 'communities' must be studied across a country-side and against a known regional and topographical background or set of milieux, but sought (as the book title implied) to draw contrasts rather than to seek direct comparisons. This approach, involving the investigation of three markedly different Cambridgeshire parishes, al-lowed scope for the use of the imagination, and permitted an intendedly holistic or 'total' approach to each parish. She wrote that she had 'deliberately chose(n) those parishes which contrasted with each other geographically, agriculturally, demographically, in the distribution of land, inheritance customs and even in the availability of schooling and their conformist or nonconformist history ... '. Here there lurked what could have been a debating point of the most crucial nature, for every locality is likely to have an element of uniqueness in it, truthful or illusory, and there is a strong case for arguing that only the most exhaustive comparative study, at a number of levels, can reveal the true distinctiveness of the places or local societies studied. However, Spufford was concerned to move the discussion forward at two more immediately manageable levels: she wished to demonstrate that the deeper and spiritual humanity of villagers could be revealed by a study of their evident religious feelings and reactions, and to show that religious bonds could cement the communal life of the localities con-cerned. She felt that Hoskins's *The Midland Peasant* approach, which largely ignored religion, placed far too heavy a stress upon economic man, who appeared as an abstraction.[20]

Spufford also warned that '"demographic man" and "literate man" remain essentially as much abstractions as "economic man". Until these different facets of human life are related, instead of being treated by separate historians, we will not have reconstructed the life of the Eng-lish villager.'[21] Here we have to recognize that the search for the local community could counteract the effects of the fragmentation mentioned, were that search to be carried on in a probing spirit – as in *Contrasting Communities* – but without fixed hypotheses determining what one expects to find. That historians should compare different levels of social linkage and activity, where it seems likely that the conditions for community could exist, is of the essence. Margaret Spufford also issued another even more important warning about attempts to 'reconstruct' the local community in detail: 'in part the task is impossible, because the source material simply does not exist'.[22] Propagandists for local history rarely dwell on the severe limitations of source material, whether in presence or absence, and more should have been made of this authoritative word of caution. Although researchers' ingenuity will yet find new means of utilizing conventional sources, the uses of such items are necessarily finite, and the medieval, Tudor and Stuart periods offer far too many methodological and interpretative challenges to the student who sets out to find real enlightenment in local history, and in the supposed community that lies at its heart.

Both Margaret Spufford's study, and that by David Hey, recognized that a local society or community was not necessarily coterminous with parish boundaries, and both authors were evidently familiar with the sociological work by W.M. Williams on 'Ashworthy' in the West Country. Williams (1963) found that farmers in his parish moved frequently to adjoining or even to more distant parishes up to eight miles away, and that these surrounding places were also, for a wider Ashworthy population, 'places where the people of the parish (had) many kindred and friends'.[23] Although Spufford and Hey were guided or influenced by the Cambridge demographers, little work had at that time been done on local migratory patterns, and both authors had to use Ashworthy as an analogy, and felt obliged to assume that similar patterns of movement (forming a 'social area') obtained in the case of Stuart parishes. This supposition or working model was undoubtedly sensible, and is now accepted as being so,[24] but it raised some uncomfortable challenges regarding the shape and spread of the local community, when the latter could not be restricted to the parish itself.

David Hey's *An English Rural Community: Myddle Under the Tudors and Stuarts* is a single-parish study, and at its heart lies a remarkable source, Richard Gough's 'Antiquityes and Memoyres of the Parish of Myddle' (written or compiled in 1701–06 and, in Hey's words, 'one of the most valuable sources for the study of late-Stuart England that one could wish to find'). Two complementary observations must be made here: such contemporary writings are conspicuous by their rarity, and yet they provide crucial evidence for the ideas of community and local identity held by men and women of that time. Gough saw his parish as a community, and recorded the latter through pew positions in the parish church. He also recognized the existence of a North Shropshire world beyond the parish – the social area already discussed.

Moreover, another difficulty appears in the administrative pattern of the parish of Myddle, a large one comprising seven townships, some of which had been (literally) hewn out of the surrounding woodland in a total parish area of nearly nine square miles. Given that much social movement was on foot, and that the inhabitants of any one township were primarily concerned with their own farms, cottage holdings and (where they existed) common rights, one is entitled to ask how much social and kinship contact they actually had with parishioners in more distant parts of their own parish, as compared with (let us say) contact with friends and kin over the nearby parish boundary.

Hey, in what is undoubtedly a fine book designed to give reasonable substance to the Leicester notion of local community, thoroughly explores the demography and the social structure of Myddle, and he is aware of the difficulties here mentioned. Unfortunately, the Leicester emphasis rested on the single parish (few local historians have been disposed to follow Margaret Spufford's multi-parish approach) and, as we shall see, even an unusually sophisticated historical anthropologist has been disposed to see the multi-township parish as a community – which it may well have been in some limited but distinct respects. But this begs a very large question, to do with regularities and frequencies of contact at varying social levels and in differing geographical situations, and the question is likely to remain, because historical records do not give us sufficient data to afford firm answers. The seriousness of the township problem is rendered more so by virtue of the fact that local historians rarely recognize it. The latter will, however, find a clear warning in Lewis's *Particular Places*:

> in the lowland counties of southern, eastern and midland England most parishes contained only one township, though there were exceptions in all regions. (Cambridgeshire is a good example). In the West Country and the North it was the single-township parish that was exceptional; most parishes had several townships and some contained very many.[25]

This fact, in reality commonplace enough, has certain challenging implications which have rarely been discussed in local historical circles. One can attempt to extricate oneself from difficulty by saying 'that is quite simply dealt with. A township in the Pennines is the equivalent of a parish in Nottinghamshire or Oxfordshire, and can be written about in much the same manner'. But is it, and can it? In an isolated part of upland England, it will indeed have a distinct separateness about it which suggests the existence of a small community, but it will also have a multitude of ties with neighbouring townships and with the main or parish church. It will, in the writer's experience, have more than one manor in the immediate vicinity during much of its history. Lewis acknowledges the implicit problems in a passage which is praiseworthy for its frankness if not for its conclusion:

> Many beginners in local history are unnecessarily confused by the complex relationship of parishes, manors and villages, to say nothing of other overlapping or intermediate units such as townships, chapelries, hundreds and rural deaneries. In fact, most local historians interested in a particular place do not have any difficulty at all; a hamlet, a village, or a group of small settlements served by a parish church normally bears a single name which expresses its unity and its identity as a community deserving separate study.[26]

It is interesting to find that a community, which changes over time, is here defined by nomenclature, which does so only glacially. The truth is that a name relates to a place, and not to a community, and the reason why many putative writers about places or localities 'do not have any difficulty at all' is simple: they are working in a state of innocence concerning the matters discussed here, even though they will quickly see the point of raising questions when given a real opportunity to do so. Meanwhile, as in this case, the community appears in the act of preconception, collection of data and writing rather than in the process of searching for the answers to developing questions. Yet, a warning against this danger and tendency had already appeared in 1977, issued by Alan Macfarlane in the journal *Social History*:

> 'communities' tend to lie in the eye and methodology of the beholder ... the method of living in an area and studying it over a number of months or years through the observation of interpersonal relationships tends to create in the observer's mind, if nowhere else, a sense of an integrated 'community'. The method tends to bring the expected results. This is reinforced because of the strong belief in the objective existence of communities ... The investigator will find community bonds and community sentiments because he expects to do so.

It is important to add that Macfarlane was here referring to anthropological as well as local historical exercises, but the essential point remains the same. He went on to explain that two skilled observers, working on a 'community' in Mexico at an interval of 15 years, had found 'two entirely different "communities" because of their differing interests'. Macfarlane added meaningly that 'it will be interesting to see whether, when the time comes to re-study Wigston Magna made famous by Hoskins, a set of entirely different conclusions will be reached'.[27]

The crude and indiscriminate use of the community concept, as surveyed here, has some major drawbacks which should be debated in any gathering of historians, amateur or professional: it has limited explanatory power; it is likely to produce some misleading representations of the roots of social change (because major social frictions and divisions are likely to be missing from the picture presented); and it hinders the more subtle and revealing uses of the same concept. The latter is very far from useless; but it is dangerous when used without the most careful qualification, and when employed without regard for the limitations of data and sources. Discovering that George A. Hillery had identified 94 different definitions of 'community', Finberg simply brushed the matter of detailed definition aside,[28] and thereby, albeit unwittingly, cut away a real theoretical base on which local history might have rested, and ignored a means by which theory and empirical research might have been brought into contact. This is a serious matter; much of local and regional history in present-day Britain is shot through with narrow empiricism. It is, after all, theory which helps the researcher to pose questions to the historical material he or she has elicited, and which helps that researcher to develop a debating language.

This is not to suggest that important developments have not taken place minus the immediate stimulus of this notional debate, and it is intriguing that during the 1970s local history did, after a long period of apparent intellectual stagnation, appear to be moving towards a critical point at which real debate might have flowered. The early part of the decade saw not only the appearance of the major works by Spufford and Hey, but also, in the following year (1975), the formation of the Social History Society and, soon after that, the interesting attempt to commence a debate by Macfarlane (already quoted). The social historians at first showed considerable interest in the organization of local historical material, if purely from an instrumental standpoint.[29] Not long afterwards, History Workshop (1976) vigorously espoused the cause of local history, bringing some intellectual acuity and energy – mainly through the writing of Raphael Samuel on behalf of an editorial collective – into what threatened to be at least a proto-debate.[30] At quite a different level, organizers in the more generalized local history interest and industry, untouched by the pristine radicalism of History Workshop (the organizers chose an eminent Tory chairman), contrived the formation of the Committee to Review Local History, the Blake Committee of 1977–79, which was preoccupied with a constructive survey of leisure-time local study and organization. Apparently for that reason, the Committee refused to be drawn into discussion of the more fundamental nature of the subject. In particular, the Committee followed Finberg exactly in refusing to take up the definition of the local community, instead settling for a catch-all and vacuous formula to embrace local history ('we venture to suggest that local history is the study of man's past in relation to his locality, locality being determined by an individual's interests and experience').[31]

Yet it is true that locality or locale, local societies or social systems, place, framework, and the different types of community all call for the most rigorous discussion, the main body of which cannot be covered in these pages. Meanwhile, the end of the 1970s brought not only the thorough but somewhat colourless and only partially effective deliberations of the Blake Committee, but also, paradoxically, another striking achievement in the local history field which did go a long way to meeting the criticisms and qualifications which appear in this book – namely, Levine and Wrightson (1979), *Poverty and Piety in an English Village.*[32]

This work had, and has, some cardinal virtues. One of the most notable resides in the rigorous analysis with which the social organization of late-Tudor and Stuart Terling in Essex was treated by the authors. This very definite structure, shown in the tables supplied with the text, means that a significant part of the authors' findings are comparable with those for localities of similar or differing nature. (Margaret Spufford's work is strong in this respect.) This is a point of crucial importance, for a basic criticism of much local historical 'community' study is that it is essentially non-comparable and non-cumulative, resembling in this respect the work of literary creation rather than of social science.[33] This lack of comparability is in part the product of a 'literariness' or literary bias which has long been present in the British local historical tradition, but it is also the consequence of the individualism that runs through this branch of study, a near-anarchism only partially redeemed by the carefully organized structure of the topographical sections of the Victoria County Histories. The latter, however, do not ask overt questions (although they may prompt a good many). Levine and Wrightson's study poses historical questions throughout, implicitly and explicitly, and it has succeeded in setting new and challenging standards in the writing of local history.

It cannot be said that this challenge has been accepted. Indeed, the book was semi-dismissed in the *Local Historian* as another contribution to the fashionable social history of the period,[34] and there is always a danger that an original piece of work may be too easily pigeon-holed because it appears to serve a passing range of interests. When this is said, however, local or localized history can be seen too comprehensively as 'social' because it is concerned with local 'societies', and this consideration needs further discussion. To return to our immediate argument, Levine and Wrightson did not, to their credit, make any assumptions about 'communities', although they were keenly aware of the importance of kin-networks in village life, and to that extent shared the approach of Alan Macfarlane and colleagues (1977a) in his near contemporary *Reconstructing Historical Communities.* Indeed, Macfarlane's book, and essay already cited, bear some relation to the Levine and Wrightson approach,[35] just as all three authors owed something to the earlier deliberations of the Cambridge Group for the Study of Population and Social Structure. Macfarlane utilized the word 'community' freely enough, but in a limited and anthropological sense; Levine and Wrightson sought evidence for a changing social structure, and also for conflict of differing and significant kinds. They constructed a picture of a social system within Terling, most certainly, but it was one which was under stress during late Tudor and Stuart decades; there was control, or the exertion of power, on the part of the landowning groups, but there was endemic conflict at all social levels. As the authors wrote, 'the village was riddled with petty conflicts'. In one important sense, too, *Piety and Poverty* went beyond Margaret Spufford's conceptualization in that its authors took account not only of religion but also of irreligion, and if 'religious man' is made to work as an important and binding element in local society, then 'dissolute and irreligious man' is there as deviant and mischief-maker. In this sense, *Poverty and Piety* moves more closely towards 'total local history' than does its precursors.

Levine and Wrightson lay much emphasis on the idea of social control, and it becomes clear that groups of people do not act in a given way by virtue of some kind of democratically agreed social contract. Their actions over time take given forms because they are trained, influenced and coerced into doing so, and religion, government and childhood training are respectively the means whereby conformity to norms of behaviour is sought. This is a well-known theme in social history, and the *Local Historian* reviewer reacted understandably if his intention was to hint that the tiny parish of Terling (with a population of 300 to 600 persons) was being used to exemplify – or was being presented as a microcosm of – a great body of English social history. The authors asserted that 'if we are to understand the convergence of forces that shaped the nation in the later sixteenth and seventeenth centuries, we must uncover the processes of change at work in the smaller worlds of county and village'.[36] Terling was a model for a much larger stage, and its historians were not looking for an organic or holistic community within its confines. Yet, essentially instrumental though their approach undoubtedly was, the authors nevertheless produced a comprehensive picture of a local society, one which merged into a much wider social area. Their concern was with change and the motors for change.

For this reason, they surveyed local society over a relatively short period, utilizing a variety of tools for the purposes of close examination; aggregation of parish register entries, family reconstitution, the analysis of large accumulations of civil and ecclesiastical court cases, classifications of landownership, and in-depth use of records of the church and of nonconformity (a severe disadvantage was a lack of available probate inventories for analysis). Their work provides as a sharp reminder of the vast investment of effort, not to mention sheer ingenuity, that present-day computerized recording and analysis requires.

Alan Macfarlane and colleagues' *Reconstructing Historical Communities* (1977a) is in some respects remarkably similar in approach, although at the time of writing (1996) a full survey report of his dual project – on Earls Colne and Kirkby Lonsdale – is not available. Macfarlane, too, was interested in the reconstruction of kinship networks from a massive database, but was also interested in the significance of many thousands of biographical or life-cycle details of the individuals that made up the network. Yet the sheer ambitiousness of the project threw some of its shortcomings into relief; as Macfarlane observed:

> a ... defect in the data is that it is almost all at the level of behaviour. Almost all of it describes events and actions, rather than thoughts and feelings. We have a very large amount of information about how people interacted, but know far too little about what they thought, felt or even said they were doing. This means that it is possible to generate very large amounts of statistical information, but the reasons as to *why* people behaved in the observed patterns are left, on the whole, to our intuition.[37]

Here Macfarlane identified the ultimate obstacle to the study of historical 'communities': there are few biographical or other sources which tell us what people's deeper sentiments of local and communal attachment actually were.

This is not the only problem arising from Macfarlane's major project in Essex and the former Westmorland. Kirkby Lonsdale is a typical Pennine or sub-Pennine parish with a major centre of population, the small market town of Kirkby Lonsdale itself, but with a total area of nearly 50 square miles. In this territory no fewer than nine townships were distributed in the seventeenth and eighteenth centuries,[38] and some were very clearly distinct from the central town, having (like Barbon, Hutton Roof, Lupton, Middleton and Mansergh) their own manors at some historical stage. While this complicating factor in no way contradicts any of Macfarlane's own arguments, which have anthropological and social historical preoccupations, it raises some enormously difficult problems for the local researcher who wishes to think and write in terms of distinctive communities: seven of the Kirkby Lonsdale townships became chapelries, with their own places of worship, and the pressures from local worshippers to seek the grant of a chapel of ease must surely say something about the growth of a sense of separateness!

Equally, however, the influence of the central town or place cannot be ignored,[39] while at the same time there is no certainty that this great parish area was also the social area for Kirkby Lonsdale proper.

Does this then mean that the study of local historical communities is useless? Much depends, after all, on the type of study pursued. Limited or unimaginative hypotheses produce equally uninspiring results, and the investigator is usually too occupied with the collection of data to worry about major debating issues. Evidence from a single parish, or even two disparate parishes, may be unsatisfactory in the resolution of many problems in social history, even though light can be thrown on major questions by single-parish investigation. Since the publication of the works discussed above, two studies in particular have demonstrated the strengths and the limitations of the single-location depth project: the Wrightson and Levine (1991) study of the large coalmining parish of Whickham on Tyneside, 1560 to 1765, and the major two-volume work by Marjorie Keniston McIntosh (1986, 1991) on the Manor and Liberty of Havering in Essex between 1200 and 1620.[40] Although each of these remarkable projects traces local historical processes of change in immense detail, neither really confronts the problems of 'community', perhaps because in early modern times each area, Whickham and Havering, was subject to considerable population movement and short-term change. The case was different in medieval Havering, where conditions making for stability were unusually marked.[41] The latter manor, however, had several centres of population within it and, therefore, contained several putative 'communities' (which are not discussed as such).

Where the nature of former communal links is never identified or tested, even by the most patently thorough scholars, then there must be a limit to fruitful discussion of the local community – save as a means of illustrating a more general social and other history. Local history clearly has to struggle beyond instrumental employment of this kind.

Notes

1. This formulation, it should be re-emphasized, was first put into currency in the 1950s; cf. Finberg (1952), *The Local Historian and His Theme*, Leicester University Press: Leicester, 9, and also W.G. Hoskins (1952), 'The Writing of Local History', *History Today*, 2, (1), 490. Accordingly, it has had a remarkably long unchallenged run.
2. Phythian-Adams (1987), *passim*.
3. Cf. Lewis, C. (1989), *Particular Places: An Introduction to English Local History*, London Library: London; Tiller, K. (1992), *English Local History: an Introduction*, Alan Sutton: Stroud.

4. Lewis, (1989), 24–7.
5. Lewis, (1989), 23.
6. Cf. the controversy in the *Amateur Historian* in 1963–64, in which the main contributions were Marshall, J.D. (1963), 'The Use of Local History: Some Comments', 6, (1), Autumn, 11–17; Read, D. (1964), 'The Use of Local History: The Local History of Modern Times', 6, (4), Summer, 121–4; and Everitt, A. (1964), 'The Study of Local History', 6, (2), 38–44.
7. The quotation is from Walsh, W.H. (1962), 'History and Theory', *Encounter*, 18, (6), 50–54.
8. Marshall, article cited in Note 6 above, and Powell, W.R. (1958), 'Local History in Theory and Practice', *Bulletin of the Institute of Historical Research*, 31, 41–8. However, it is important to recognize that sociologists were carrying on a parallel but much more searching discussion of 'community' in the 1950s and 1960s, and much of this is reflected in Frankenberg, R. (1966 and later edns), *Communities in Britain: Social Life in Town and Country* (Penguin Original). Had local historians been disposed to study twentieth-century history, they would have absorbed much of this discussion, and would have known that Stacey M. (1960), the author of *Tradition and Change: A Study of Banbury*, Cambridge University Press: Cambridge, ruthlessly dissected the limitations of the community concept (1969) in 'The Myth of Community Studies', *British Journal of Sociology*, 20, 134–45. Not surprisingly, the 'community' debate slackened in the following decade, but it has now re-emerged as a set of intense exchanges on the nature of 'locality'; see in particular the journal *Antipode, passim* from *circa* 1980.
9. Finberg, H.P.R. (1962), 'Local History', in H.P.R. Finberg (ed.) *Approaches to History*, Routledge: London, 116.
10. Finberg (1962), 121.
11. Finberg (1962), 118.
12. Ibid.
13. Ibid.
14. Addy, J. (1989) *Sin and Society in the Seventeenth Century*, Routledge: London. Dr Addy, for example, tells us (p. 199) that what made church courts unpopular 'was their attempt to enforce moral standards of conduct'! This book seems to suggest that association within the Anglican church was not necessarily of a spiritual nature. See especially Thomas, K. (1971) *Religion and the Decline of Magic*, Cambridge University Press: Cambridge, 6, on 'Religion and the People', especially 160–5. Every local historian should read this survey.
15. Lewis, c. (1989), *Particular Places*, 27.
16. Hawley, A. (1950), *Human Ecology: A Theory of Community Structure*, Ronald Press: New York. See in particular his comments on 'The Community as an Organism', 50 ff. 'Youth, maturity and senescence' are stressed. See also Bell, C. and Newby, H. (1971), *Community Studies: An Introduction to the Sociology of the Local Community*, Allen and Unwin: London, 32 ff.
17. Finberg (1962), 119.
18. Parker, C. (1990), *The English Historical Tradition*, John Donald: Edinburgh, 236.
19. Parker (1990), 237.

20. Spufford, M. (1973), 'The Total History of Village Communities', *Local Historian*, 10, (8), November, 398–401. The lengthy quotation is from p. 399.

21. Spufford, (1973), 400. But see also Macfarlane, A. (with Harrison, S. and Jardine, C. (1977a), *Reconstructing Historical Communities*, Cambridge University Press: Cambridge, 192–3.

22. Spufford, (1973), 401.

23. Williams, W.M. (1963), *A West Country Village; Ashworthy*, Routledge: London, 38–9, 79, 109.

24. Levine, D., and Wrightson, K. (1979), *Poverty and Piety in an English Village: Terling, 1525–1700*, Academic Press: London, 74 ff., are, for example, quite clear about the significance of the social area.

25. Lewis, C. (1989), 22–3.

26. Ibid.

27. Macfarlane, A. , (1977b), 'The Study of Communities', *Social History*, 5, May, 631–2, 634–5.

28. Finberg (1962), 117.

29. Evidence for this temporary preoccupation is to be found in the earliest Social History Newsletters issued by the society in 1975–76.

30. The main contributions from History Workshop (apart from a number of interesting community-type studies) took the form of discussion articles by Samuel, R. e.g. (1976), 'Local History and Oral History', *History Workshop Journal*, (1), Spring, 191–208; and *idem* (1979), 'Urban History and Local History', *History Workshop Journal*, (8), Autumn, iv–vi. Both essays are highly perceptive, but represent an interesting re-run of the left-wing campaign to influence local history in the 1950s, and an over-optimistic inability to perceive the intractable nature of the local history industry. Much more recently, Samuel has become a total partisan on behalf of the latter and of popular antiquarianism generally; see Appendix to this book, below.

31. Report of the Committee to Review Local History (Blake Committee) (1979), 2.01–2.03.

32. For the full title of this work, see Note 24 above.

33. Macfarlane (1977b), 637.

34. The review in question (by Rogers, A., 1980), in the *Local Historian*, 14, (4), 245, was both perceptive and accurate (it assessed *Poverty and Piety* as 'a notable contribution to local historical studies'), and implied that it represented a fashionable approach to social history – also truthful enough. But the matter of comparability was not taken up, nor were local historians urged to read the book!

35. The historians discussed here took part in a seminar organized by Macfarlane at King's College, Cambridge, in the winter of 1975–76. The gathering was called to explore the possibilities of social and anthropological history based on local research, and those present included Margaret Spufford, Mary Prior, David Levine, Keith Wrightson and the present writer.

36. Levine and Wrightson (1979), 1.

37. Macfarlane (1977b), 646.

38. For the organization of the parish of Kirkby Lonsdale, see Moon, M. (1851), *A History, Topography and Directory of Westmorland etc.*, (reprint, Whitehaven, 1978), Mannex: Beverley, 347–62.

39. For the influence of market towns in Cumbria, see Marshall, J.D. (1983), 'The Rise and Transformation of the Cumbrian Market Town 1660–1900', *Northern History*, 19, especially 149. Kirkby Lonsdale was in the Lancaster and Kendal spheres of influence in the eighteenth century.

40. McIntosh, M.K. (1986), *Autonomy and Community: The Royal Manor of Havering, 1200–150*, Cambridge University Press: Cambridge; *idem* (1991), *A Community Transformed: The Manor and Liberty of Havering, 1500–1620*, Cambridge University Press: Cambridge; Wrightson, K. and Levine, D. (1991), *The Making of an Industrial Society: Whickham, 1560–1765*, Oxford University Press: Oxford.

41. McIntosh (1986), *passim*. It should be said that both the McIntosh and the Levine and Wrightson studies deploy an astonishing range of source material, and one is reminded that it is unusual for most parishes or manors to be covered in such detail.

CHAPTER FIVE

Beyond the Single Place

If the local historian is not simply concerned with 'the local community' (in the singular), then with what should his or her proper preoccupation be? Until the 1960s, the Leicester scholars gave their attention largely to the single local community. In that decade, however, there was a significant broadening of stress, in that the 'county community', as seen by Everitt,[1] received much more attention. Thus a source of great potential confusion was created, because main authorities on the theory of historic communities, such as Hillery[2] and König,[3] do not mention the idea of the county (or a similar administrative unit in the USA or in the European mainland) as being a suitable space for community study. Consideration of the county (or shire) surely entails the study of multiple 'communities' of greatly differing magnitudes, as related to complex societies.[4]

In this chapter, we shall consider how far territories wider than the parish or township but smaller than the county can be distinguished for separate examination but also related one to the other within a broader historical and spatial framework, and how effectively such local societies can be broken into larger and smaller units. This will necessarily, at a later stage (Chapter 6), lead to the consideration of the idea of place.

What is clear is that the concept of place – which cannot be taken as equivalent to the idea of community – is unlikely to be seriously regarded when the community concept is so frequently and elastically invoked. Hence, Frankenberg (1966), in a well-known and popular study, has had no inhibitions about applying the term 'community' to a noticeably wide variety of settlements and urban entities. It becomes clear that the term is in fact a catch-all one, used *inter alia* to represent, in the words of G.J. Lewis, 'the smallest spatial system which encompasses the major features of society'.[5] Another view is concerned with psychological or cultural bonding on the part of inhabitants. It is certainly true that students of local history often assume that the historical folk-village,[6] or the English parish, nurtures a special kind of closeness of relationship between individuals. Hence, even so imaginative a commentator on local history as Samuel has been drawn to the idea of the village community: 'social relations in a village are, in some sort transparent, and the individual does bear some close relationship to the whole'.[7]

However, argued Samuel, 'the appearance of oneness presented (or assumed) by local historians is often deceptive'. Moreover, modern

urban history presents very real problems: 'in a borough ... the structure is no longer the clearly repeated cells of the honeycomb, but
something altogether more complicated and hard to grasp'.[8] Here, in
relatively straightforward language, Samuel was making the familiar
distinction between the idea of the *Gemeinschaft*, the supposed historical community of being, blood and locality[9] as seen by Tönnies over a
century ago, and the *Gesellschaft*, the social world of rational, market-
oriented, open, but often contractual relationships.[10] Now, it is tempting to suggest that local history, as *history*, ends with the appearance of
this latter atomized world, because there are few concrete local and
social organisms, of a semi-permanent and easily interconnected kind,
which can be safely traced and analysed in the large town or city.
Indeed, the intractability of this 'complicated and hard to grasp' world
could be advanced as a defence of the noticeable tendency to bring local
history to a close in the mid-nineteenth century or by 1914.

Reflection will show that this apparent impasse is brought about by
the obsession of local historians with the single local, social and spatial
unit (seen as a 'community'). This concentration upon the single unit
has meant that the local researcher has been unable to study sequences
of events (or patterns of behaviour) of a particular kind across a varied
countryside or urban area, and so form conclusions on social movements across the territory in which the events take place. Repeated
patterns of behaviour will often point to the possible existence of close
social relationships within the ostensibly separate places in which they
occur, and the former may even ultimately appear as community characteristics. It is also likely that the investigator cannot begin to understand possible community characteristics within a town or city until he
or she widens his or her focus in the manner suggested. In other words,
the investigator is obliged sooner or later to adopt a comparative approach, an assumption which is borne out by the methodologies used
by some social historians in regional historical journals, or in *Past and
Present*.[11]

It is argued here, however, that the researching local historian should
draw his or her examples from a given territory in the hope of defining
their characteristics more clearly. What generally happens now is that a
researcher will draw examples from a rather vaguely defined area because they happen to support his or her thesis, sometimes using county
data as a matter of convenience. As is well known (but not very often
recognized), the investigator using scattered examples of behaviour or
institutional activity across a territory may sooner or later be accused of
falling foul of the 'ecological fallacy', whereby it has been stated that
statistical aggregates (from a variety of places) cannot be held to explain the behaviour of individuals.[12] The only conceivable answer to

psychology of individuals

this problem is supplied by thorough knowledge of the history and development of the places that are used as 'ecological' examples, in such a way that genuine light is thrown on the psychology of individuals and groups and on their likely motivation – difficult though the organization of such information may prove to be. Meanwhile, many of the users of regional historical examples probably run the risk of falling into the ecological fallacy, because it is extremely difficult to obtain evidence relating to the circumstances influencing the behaviour of individuals in given places and milieux.

A possible or seeming contradiction arises here. The argument implies that the student of local history should be interested not in one place, but in several places, and even in a region, for their own respective sakes. In fact, the localist or regionalist can only make sense of the complex historical panorama before him or her by concentrating on certain themes and approaches which make comparison possible, and different approaches will actually focus attention on different places. This investigator is nevertheless to be distinguished from others who use a regional approach, in that he or she is consciously searching for cumulative links and interconnections within a region and, in establishing norms of behaviour or types of change for given periods, he or she is ascertaining what is typical and, just as importantly, atypical in given localities. The 'behaviour' concerned may be demographic, political or economic, and the historian's overriding aim may be that of the search for norms, but may be just as distinctly the broad explanation of the timing and form of actions and events – and the possible connection of one with another in a given place or group of places.

each place contrasted with another place

The study of individual places may indeed produce suggestive discoveries and ideas, but the former will not yield more than a thumbnail sketch of what is likely to happen in the wider and surrounding society. Where there is variety of documentation, an individual place is always likely to appear unique unless the contrary is clearly demonstrated.

Need the places

Meanwhile, the surrender and displacement of the individual place-study – hardly likely in the light of current fashions and trends – may signify also the end of the narrative or biographical approach to local history, whereby a story covering centuries is unfolded stage by stage. It is this element of story-telling which appeals to large numbers of devotees, who unquestionably instruct themselves in some rudiments of history when engaged in collecting and composition. There can also be little doubt that there is a function for narrative in good historical writing,[13] just as it is certain that there are themes for narration within regional history. Narrative, however, must be built on a sure foundation of case studies, and it is the latter which have been lacking or defective. Similarly, it has already been observed that the Leicester-inspired local histories of weight and merit, like those by Spufford and Hey, concentrate on relatively short periods and on case studies within periods. Local history faces the abandonment of the extended narrative if it is to be at all worthy of respect and, as new branches of specialization take effect, the prospect of the development of local history as a higher branch of story-telling becomes more remote.

One other attraction of local history resides in its supposed power to take the reader close to the experiences of everyday life within some (if not all) periods. The history of a locality is ostensibly the history of the humble people in that locality, in so far as their lives are fairly portrayed in the available documents. In fact, the power of such evocation residing in immediately local documents is often both patchy and limited and, in any event, it is the broad case study that digs deepest into common experience. Illustrative material from a wide territory, a countryside or a region nearly always gives richer results because of its greater reach and surer multiplication of instances, and it is still possible to relate that material to given places without surrendering solidity of evidence and soundness of deduction – given that the danger of the ecological fallacy is not forgotten.

There is the further point that everyday life spreads historically across a wide space, in that its routines and observances have been closely replicated in areas outside the main places, but also because towns and urban areas were spreading widely in their effective social reach by the middle of the nineteenth century. For the rest, everyday life is deeply influenced by economic and social patterns which are best traced regionally, i.e. through the industrial (or agrarian) region wherever that concept is relevant within the terms of modern history.

However, none of this argument for generalization and comparison disposes of or side-lines the case for so-called depth study of particular places within a region. The powerful advantage of local history, as local history, is that a mass of varied information – economic, sociological, political, religious, administrative – can be *synthesized* and combined in the pursuit of basic arguments, questions and themes, and only in certain fields or departments can more generalized regional comparisons be effectively sustained. The case for locality study is still notably powerful, because it affords a view of the working of a local society in the round. The work of defining types of locality represents a major challenge and discussion which is developed in Chapter 6. All that is argued here is that the in-depth study of individual places can be powerfully justified, always provided that those places are set within a general framework of information relating to a relevant neighbourhood, subregion or region. Commonly, as we have seen, the 'region' utilized is a county or even a group of counties,[14] and the smaller agrarian sub-region of the *pays*, discussed by the Leicester scholars and their followers,[15] has in practice hardly ever prompted thorough research in British conditions.[16] Indeed, there have been few convincingly viewed types of locality and sub-region between the parish and the county.

Phythian-Adams has constructed a succession of such areas in ascending order, commencing with the local 'community', going through to the neighbourhood ('dynastic' or other), and then rising to the *pays*, and thereafter to the 'over-arching society of the shire' (which may not be exactly coterminous with the administrative county). More tentatively, he has written of 'wider provincial contexts'.[17] A main assumption in his discussion is that the wider 'society' overlaps with the spatially narrower one but that each society is nevertheless recognizable to its own members. This concept of mutual or general recognition within spaces and social layers, which is not in fact directly discussed, is crucial, and a cardinal task for the local historian is not that of imposing idealized or preconceived localities on historical material, but of attempting to discover how contemporaries saw their own regional social groupings. Next, it can be forcefully argued that these divisions or spaces may very well get in the way where the tracing of historical processes is concerned, and that it is a most dangerous error to wish to confine economic, social or other historical activity within any set of preconceived social boundaries. It is safer to commence one's researches within divisions that are recognized as wholly arbitrary, using spatial areas purely for purposes of measurement and comparison, and letting the wider areas of social influence appear in the course of further investigation.

In any case, since county areas are frequently used precisely for such purposes of measurement, we may well ask what 'the over-arching society of the shire' actually means at successive stages in history, and whether the argument is really concerned with centres of power and influence – local market centres, local landed estates (whose rulers are also part of 'shire society'), the owners of great houses and their larger estates, merchant groups within larger towns and, not least, centres of major industrial activity and those who promoted the latter. The activities of such persons certainly reached out into variable and decidedly irregular spaces which often had little to do with the shape of a given county.

Meanwhile, the question of power, or coercion, is surely a crucial one, because such power will always be likely to shape the course of local events in the short term. (Regional societies and cultures, whose boundaries remain largely undefined, provide the *longues durées* which have influenced the assumptions behind some aspects of regional everyday life in the long term.) Moreover, 'power and influence' does not reside merely in the hands of individuals, but within – as need hardly be stressed – social structures and administrative mechanisms. The organizational frameworks of the parish, hundred, poor law union and county are of interest for this reason, just as the development of collective activity in society generally provides its own centres of power. However, to relate the latter to administrative areas alone is likely to be fruitless. County 'society' and county-based activities provide, at best, a convenient symbolism and sphere of operations for local military hierarchies, useful organizing areas for sports, and meeting points for the wealthy or influential. County-related symbolism has little direct relevance to the patterns of interlinked gentry and to other social and familial relationships which can be shown to have obtained in a county area *and* outside it at a given period, and much depends on the nature of allegiance to territory that is felt at that stage. A gentleman's 'country' need not be a county or a shire, a likelihood that has been obscured by the long debate on county 'communities' in the seventeenth century.[18] Clearly, the relationship of gentry families to given areas of countryside, and even to specific places, calls for the most diligent research, and it cannot be assumed that consciousness of place or territory is most fully represented at the main social meeting points recognized by the regional gentry.

Interestingly, the debate on county communities has focused at different times on the organization of military power and factions within counties, and on the related power of great houses and estates – but it has not sought to define power and influence in all their variations through time within the spaces concerned, just as it has given little attention to the subordinate social groups and classes which lay nearer the base of the social pyramid. These, it would appear, are not part of the county 'community', or are merely ancillary to it. Are we then led to suppose that habitually used or occupied areas become wider, or larger, as we ascend the social ladder? This proposition does not seem unreasonable, given that affluent persons are *ipso facto* more mobile, but it is erroneous to assume that the gentry necessarily concentrated their leisure time amusements and functions in the county town. As Clive Holmes has argued, they made increasing use of London if they had their seats in a county like Lincolnshire.[19] The county town of Lincoln, even in the nineteenth century, had a social reach, for gentry gatherings, of about 20 miles only.[20]

A county administrative organism or area, it must be agreed, has very great uses as a laboratory for study, but little is to be gained by assuming that it is in some way, at some level, a socially homogeneous unit (even if one tries to obtain more latitude by calling it a 'shire'). The single-unit (or single-place) approach to the county may have statistical and methodological advantages[21] for certain kinds of macro-economic study, but it is in other ways as full of pitfalls as the study of the isolated local community. There is much room for detailed study of socially coherent areas within counties, and here Phythian-Adams has some interesting things to say, although even he does not stress the major research difficulties that historians must face if they are to set about the work of identifying these areas. As has already been emphasized, the successive spaces between the small locality, or parish, and the major county unit, are almost a *terra incognita*, and the separate study of urban history has done little to solve this problem. In other words, towns have been studied separately from their hinterlands, even though Phythian-Adams has concluded that

> a town *plus its immediate vicinity* ... might be regarded as simply the most concentrated form of local 'society' (with its own component 'communities' – parochial or occupational – and its own dynastic neighbourhoods which are either connected to the surrounding countryside, or even, if it is large enough, restricted to the town's own inhabited confines, including the suburbs).[22]

This promising idea has been generally evaded or ignored by students of urban history, perhaps because plain 'urbanity' offers less trouble than urban influence running through a variety of shades of grey, and so the more subtle social divisions of localities, large areas and regions are mainly unexplored. Meanwhile, the idea of the local town as a centre of influence in larger countrysides remains an important one in all stages of modern history, as the present writer (Marshall, 1983) argued in *Northern History*.

Such a town-centred area of influence, with social linkages forged by the very processes of urbanization, is clearly likely to be a basic unit in any kind of wider study of regions, but this form of social area, or 'society', has its own shapes and uniquenesses, and it seems much simpler to compare and combine more basic units like townships or parishes. The further conclusion would seem to be that there is nothing to discountenance the use of parish data for the study of a town's social area and that, indeed, the employment of such data is crucial. It is true that such an area will change over time and that, accordingly, it is best studied within an even broader framework of parish and sub-regional data. The writer's own term for such a social area is that of the *public setting*, in the sense that the latter provides a background or general territory for the activities of a majority of the relevant population at a given time. It will remain true that areas of movement tend, as has been noted, to be class-specific as well as occupationally related, and that the more affluent groups have ranged across comparatively wider areas over time. However, this does not alter the likelihood that the public setting has provided a theatre or territory for the activities of most people, whether industrially or agriculturally employed, but that any such setting will overlap heavily with its neighbour – the overlap meaning that a significant number of people in a peripheral locality will have a choice of two or more market or urban centres instead of one.

This discussion points towards a crystallization, namely the certainty that in ideal circumstances a historian has to choose a psychologically or sociologically coherent area which is constantly changing in shape, but which does reflect a form of collective consciousness at any given time. Alternatively, the investigator must stay initially within the confines of a fixed area – one administratively pre-chosen for him or her, or, as a further variant, an area which he or she has decided upon for a given research purpose, and which may or may not follow convenient administrative boundaries of a useful kind. These thoughts have bearing on the idea of place and its validity for given purposes, and this key topic is discussed in Chapter 6.

The foregoing discussion has raised some major conceptual problems. Implicit within it is a sense that as understanding and knowledge increase, new insights into local history, comparative and other, will be forthcoming. In other words, it is assumed that such understanding and knowledge will be *cumulative* at some crucial points. However, the writing of history, local and other, has been essentially individualistic, and so any insights into a broader or regional framework of study have depended upon accidents of choice, fashion and (sometimes) regional organization of clubs, societies and academic activity.

Organized discussion of individual historic regions has depended on still embryonic academic initiatives,[23] and notwithstanding the important function of several avowedly regional or provincially related academic journals,[24] there is little debate touching on the problems raised in this chapter and the two following. Yet the case for such debate is surely irrefutable: if that amorphous entity known as 'the nation' can provide a theatre for discourse, so can its individual regions and localities. Through an examination of the parts, we may yet derive more understanding of the whole. However, such a truth is clearly not self-evident, and any apparent complacency regarding its implications is partly explained by two factors: the vast amount of antiquarian and proto-historical accumulation at the level of the historic and the administrative county, expressed through learned society articles and transactions; and the related tendency by publishers and writers to commission and produce county chronicles.[25] Hudson clearly had these publications in mind when she observed that 'the region has too often been used as a convenient box into which masses of descriptive material is stuffed',[26] and the aspiration of such productions is largely that of combining quantities of disparate subject-matter chronologically under a series of general headings purporting to deal with the effects of geographical factors, changes on the land, changes by period, the influence of gentry families and industrialists, changes in transport and so on. The narrative is the style of presentation adopted, and the general approach is that of conflating what is available in the form of transactions articles, existing books, theses and occasional items in specialist periodicals, with a necessary use of county archives in the more ambitious cases.

The broad assumption throughout is that such a survey is best left to the interested and knowledgeable individual, who alone can give some kind of unity to his or her treatment of the county's history. Such publications do have primal value, in that they pull together for inspection what is broadly known and, if the author is an experienced historian, he or she can go well beyond this level and point to major themes and questions, thus encouraging further debate. However, the general tendency of the conventional chronicler is far removed from this. His or her aim seems to be that of supplying information in such a manner as to kill curiosity and questions together, except in the case of individuals with highly specific interests. Clearly, then, such publications are essentially inert.

The last half-century, however, has seen a heavy multiplication of university theses and dissertations with local and regional significance and subject-matter – some 700 of these (1946–85) have been traced for Lancashire and Cumbria alone,[27] many of them containing local social, urban, economic and political history of real quality. It is plainly already beyond the capacity of any one individual to weld this vast mass of research into a major over-arching survey of the regions concerned, and the challenge of some kind of co-operative scholarship is forced into the agenda of historians. The challenge itself transcends mere antiquarian and bibliographical compilation, and clearly embodies themes, question-positing and the organization of ideas. We are here forced to recognize that the accumulation is not one of detail only, and that it must find expression in a constantly re-forming pattern of ideas, these in turn influencing the organization of local and regional knowledge in general as relating to places and localities – with the latter connecting to a wider region.

Such an organization of ideas and information provides the *regional context which is so essential to the development of local history*. The study of the single village or the single town has – where history is seriously pursued – been related vaguely and sometimes misleadingly to a wider national picture, thus inventing a context which is so broad as to be almost meaningless. The single local example, be it Myddle or Terling, is likely to be elevated to a position of general significance, even though the authors themselves are fully aware of the importance of regional context. Phythian-Adams is right to relate local history to areas ascending in size,[28] and perhaps it is a waste of time to be diverted into too close a definition of the areas themselves. A small, sub-parish or parish-type area may be classified as of the first order; a modest town, neighbourhood or district as belonging to the second; a county or compact industrial region as belonging to the third; and a province (or European region) as belonging to the fourth. The area of the nation state (or major ethnic territory like Wales) constitutes a fifth order, and a land mass like the continent of Europe a sixth. It is clear, meanwhile, and possibly axiomatic, that any one order of local historical area should be related by the researcher to the broader area or areas immediately above it in the ascending scale, because otherwise the historian will have no close context in which to work. Much, of course, will depend upon the theme or topic pursued, and it may be that a local or sub-regional topic could be shown to have world significance.

It remains true that historical territories tend to define themselves in practical or heuristic terms, simply because archives and bibliographies are likely to dictate the agenda and scope of research. This likelihood is particularly strong in the case of county archive repositories, which in the main relate to the administrative county or to its boroughs (the latter often having their own library and sometimes archive collections). Bibliographical lists, at the county or regional level, reflect the weight and inertia of antiquarianism, providing references to a multitude of fragmented and scattered pieces of information bearing on classified topics. The information there set out does not amount to an *historical* framework, and there are strong arguments for the constant co-operation of librarian bibliographers and historians, in order that regional bibliographies, reflecting the growth of received historical frameworks, can do justice to the themes and ideas that emerge in the course of time. It is here argued that local and regional historians desperately need to keep under constant review the idea of the *received historical framework* as relating to a given place, area or territory.

This concept is an important one, and the framework itself will be composed of a number of key elements. The most basic of the latter will concern the bare evidence for the existence of a village, locality or town over several centuries, or for longer, and the main outlines of such social and other transformations which have taken place. The next element will consist of knowledge of agrarian and economic fundamentals and types of activity relating to the place or region concerned, and the third will be a highly variable record of efforts to organize analytical knowledge of these fundamentals by historians. The fourth and most important will consist of any conclusions from attempts to classify and analyse social and political behaviour and culture patterns in the place or region concerned.

This conceptualization will suggest that few places in England, or the world, have a satisfactorily evolved, received historical framework. Many places, on the other hand, have masses of inert or antiquarian data relating to them and many, too, have background information that goes far towards the filling-out of the first two elements. But ideas, at the present time, tend to come from broader and national debates, and it is chance (and occasional inspiration) that dictates their fruitful application at the regional or local level. The locality is then used as a quarry, and its interpretation may not develop in a systematic way. In this sense, received frameworks grow unevenly or ineffectually.

This criticism relates not simply to the inadequacy of antiquarian data. It bears even more strongly on the organization of local and regional knowledge, which is likely to be effectively categorized and classified only after much study and discussion. In this respect, one can only deplore the inadequacy of many local and regional bibliographies, which give little guidance as to the subject-matter of books and articles (save, perhaps, through the happy accident of a full or illuminating title), and which certainly say little about the stage reached in the evolution of the framework for any area or locality. For the rest, Grigg has put a detailed argument for regarding regionalization – and, by implication, the study of all regions – as analogous to classification in the creation of concepts of regional systems.[29] The point and purpose of this is that of creating statistics for analysis, and there is probably a case for part-constructing bibliographies in these terms. It is true that the immediate organization of regional historical study will vary in emphasis and strength over given periods. Meanwhile, some meritorious examples of surveys of regional literature give cause for encouragement,[30] while the existence of regional and provincial journals provides a ready medium for the study of regions for their own sake, rather than as instrumental in the study of broader historical questions. The comparative study of regions, too, should fall within the scope of such journals, but examples are very rare, and only the economic studies by C.H. Lee, of census regions and counties,[31] stand out in this respect. Yet such original enterprises provide new bibliographical as well as methodological insights.

In other words, historic British regions are rarely discussed by historians, who have traditionally left their (non-historical) definition to geographers and planners. The inference here is plain: there has been an unwillingness to discuss regional frameworks of differing kinds or to consider, save in passing, the interrelationships of places within regions. That historians and geographers should remain aloof from each other (when their fields of activity, especially in historical geography, often coincide, and when they can only gain from co-operation) is a regrettable consequence of the departmentalization, specialization and fragmentation of interests that has already been touched upon.

This chapter, then, has stressed the importance of historical and spatial context – usually, where the local historian is concerned, that of the region or sub-region. If the latter is engaged in the writing of a study of a single place, the broader context becomes more and not less important: the researcher must be aware of general population movements, of the wider horizons of new and old occupations, and of the more extensive occurrences of agrarian practices, social attitudes, customs and political movements. Only through such wider schemes of reference can the local investigator learn to attach significance to what he or she finds within his or her smaller compass, and to begin to explain the chronology of what is encountered there. What is demanded here is not as daunting as may appear; a general sense of what is more broadly relevant can make the work of any competent local historian markedly easier, and his or her own discoveries may serve to draw attention to the likely significance of much broader movements in a given area. What is ideally needed is a counterpoint of discovery between the localist and the regionalist. It is a fallacy to imagine that one can exist satisfactorily without the other.

The fuller or more precise definition of place, or region, calls for further comment.

Notes

1. Everitt, A.M. (1966), *The Community of Kent and the Great Rebellion*, Leicester University Press: Leicester; *idem*, (1969), *The Local Community and the Great Rebellion*, Historical Association: London, *passim*.
2. Hillery, G.A. Jr (1968), *Communal Organizations: A Study of Local Societies*, University of Chicago Press: Chicago and London, *passim*.
3. König, R. (1968), *The Community*, trans. E. Fitzgerald, Routledge: London, *passim*.
4. Hillery (1968), ch. 8, table 77, 64–72.
5. Frankenberg, R. (1966), *Communities in Britain: Social Life in Town and Country*, Penguin: Harmondsworth, *passim*; Lewis, G.J. (1979), *Rural Communities*, David and Charles, Newton Abbot, 37.
6. Hillery (1968), 27–40.
7. Samuel, R. (1979), 'Urban History and Local History', *History Workshop Journal*, (8), Autumn v.
8. Ibid.
9. Tönnies, F. (1955) *Community and Society* (Gemeinschaft and Gesellschaft, trans. C.P. Loomis), Routledge: London and New York. For a consideration of Tönnies, see Hillery (1968), 77.
10. Hillery (1968), 79–80.

11.   The main regional journals in Britain are *Northern History* (1966, the most senior in terms of duration), *Northern Scotland, Midland History* and *Southern History*, together with the *Journal of Regional and Local Studies* (published by Humberside University). Cross-regional, as distinct from intra-regional, comparisons are rare. Regionally related comparative studies are also uncommon even in *Past and Present*, perhaps the most striking example being based on French data; Jones, P.M. (1981), 'Parish, Seigneurie and the Community of Inhabitants in Southern Central France during the Eighteenth and Nineteenth Centuries, *Past and Present*, 91, 74–108. This in part relates community cohesion to geographical base, *département* by *département*, and to the concentrations or diffusions of dwellings encountered in localities, but also points to a saving cohesion offered through parishes by the church. A remarkable theoretical paper showing interplace linkages in the Weald is that by Lord, E. (1991), 'The Boundaries of Local History: A Discussion Paper', *Journal of Regional and Local Studies*, 2, (1–2), 75–84. For a most ingenious micro-study, see Rollison, D. (1981), 'Property, Ideology and Popular Culture in a Gloucestershire Village, 1660–1740', *Past and Present*, 93, 70–97. This is unusual in demonstrating community consciousness in action. For the use of 'emblematic' examples, see the same author's (1992) *The Local Origins of Modern Society, Gloucestershire, 1500–1800*, Routledge: London.

12.   This problem was initially raised by Robinson, W.S. (1950), 'Ecological Correlation and the Behaviour of Individuals', *American Sociological Review*, 15, 351–7. See, for a more recent comment, Agnew, J.A. (1987), *Place and Politics: The Geographical Mediation of the State and Society*, Allen and Unwin: Boston, 231; the danger of the ecological fallacy, discussed here, is a problem for local and regional historians in Britain.

13.   As regards narrative, see Hobsbawm, E.J. (1980) 'The Revival of Narrative: Some Comments', *Past and Present*, 86, February, 3–8, whereby L. Stone is criticized for pointing to a revival of narrative, which is held to be closely associated with right-wing or 'antiquarian empiricist' writing. The argument put in the present text refuses to associate narrative wholly with right-wing history; after all, narrative can be based on detailed study and analysis, like the work of Hobsbawm himself. For the rest, the great bulk of the British public will simply not read history which is purely analytical, a point which is overlooked.

14.   Cross-county comparisons, or those utilizing groups of counties, are rare, and are perhaps best represented in the economic comparisons of Lee, C.H. (1986), *The British Economy since 1700*, Cambridge University Press: Cambridge. See also Lee (1971), *Regional Growth in the United Kingdom since the 1880s*, McGraw-Hill: Maidenhead; *idem* (1980), 'Regional Structural Change in the Long Run: Britain 1841–1971', in S. Pollard (ed.), *Region und Industrialisierung: Studien zur Rolle der Region in der Wirtschaftsgeschichte der letzten zwei Jahrhunderts*, Vandenhoeck and Ruprecht: Göttingen. *The Regional History of England* Series, published by Longman, utilizes seemingly arbitrary combinations of counties and districts to represent the West Midlands, the East Midlands, and so on.

15.   Phythian-Adams (1987), *Rethinking Local History*, Department of English Local History Occasional Paper, No. 1, Leicester University Press: Leicester, 8–14, 24–5.

16. There are few thorough British studies of the *pays*, which seems to be defined mainly in the sub-divisions of territory of *The Agrarian History of England*. The current concept of this type of homogeneous rural area derives from Vidal de la Blache and his school of French geographers of the early twentieth century, although, objectively, the *pays* has been known for much longer; see Dickinson, R.E. (1964), *City and Region*, Routledge: London, 451–2. The late Professor Dickinson, who had read de la Blache, did not see the *pays* as necessarily homogeneous, but as the territory related to a central town.

17. Phythian-Adams (1987), 44–5.

18. Cf., for example, Blackwood, B.G. (1978), analysis of gentry endogamy in such counties as Hertfordshire, Essex, Norfolk, Suffolk, Lancashire, Cheshire, Cumberland and Westmorland, in *The Lancashire Gentry and the Great Rebellion, 1640–1660*, Chetham Society: Manchester, 25, 26.

19. Holmes, C. (1980), *Seventeenth Century Lincolnshire*. History of Lincolnshire Series, 7, History of Lincolnshire Committee: Lincoln, 79.

20. Olney, R.J. (1979), *Rural Society and County Government in Nineteenth Century Lincolnshire*; History of Lincolnshire Series, 10, History of Lincolnshire Committee: Lincoln, 14.

21. See Note 14 above.

22. Phythian-Adams (1987), 48.

23. The main initiatives have come from members of the Conference of Teachers of Regional and Local History (CORAL), a body formed in 1978–79 but, in a more territorially restricted sense, from a number of regional history study centres in the former Wolverhampton Polytechnic, the former Brighton Polytechnic, the universities of East Anglia, Lancaster, Nottingham, Exeter and Keele, with some significant moves in Teesside and Humberside, and with recent possible additions in Bangor and the present Metropolitan University, Manchester.

24. See Note 11 above.

25. Perhaps the most notable current example of county chronicling is in the form of the Darwen County History Series published by Phillimore.

26. Hudson, P. (ed.) (1989), *Regions and Industries: A Perspective on the Industrial Revolution in Britain*, Cambridge University Press: Cambridge, 21.

27. This figure is calculated from data given by Lawler, U.R.E. (1981), *North-Western Theses and Dissertations, 1950–1978*, Occasional Paper, Centre for NW Regional Studies, University of Lancaster: Lancaster; with a Supplement, 1988. It has to be concluded that the total output of such regional theses for Britain must amount to three or four thousands for the same period.

28. Phythian-Adams, (1987), 44–5.

29. Grigg, D. (1967), 'Regions, Models and Classes', in R.J. Chorley, and P. Haggett, *Integrated Models in Geography*, 473, 485. Grigg argued for a J.S. Mill type of classification, leading to logical analysis of all regional phenomena.

30. A good example of what can be achieved in the way of a provincial and also a regional publications survey is to be found in *Northern History* and its annual 'Review of Periodical Literature and Occasional Publications', edited by G.C.F. Forster.

31. Lee, C.H. (1971, 1980, 1986).

CHAPTER SIX

Space, Place and Region

The very concept of a received historical framework, as discussed in the previous chapter, implies that the study of local and regional history must be *cumulative*, first in an obvious sense of the multiplication of locally relevant facts and instances and, more subtly but less certainly, in the sense that the sheer process of accumulation will bring wisdom and insight in its train. However, any uncertainty about the emergence of these qualities is best set aside until we have established conditions in which the localist and regionalist alike can work more efficiently, using a framework of knowledge which is at once both spatial and temporal. Nearly all scholars working in the regional and local fields seem to cherish a deep faith that their own particular accumulations will represent pebbles deposited upon a mountain of useful knowledge, and this applies to antiquaries as well as to historians.

It may be unhappily true that accumulation of any kind sooner or later brings diminishing returns, and it is for this reason that the importance of criticism, debate and contention is stressed in the present argument. We have drawn attention to the almost total absence of debate in many parts of the local historical field, and this relates especially to matters of conceptualization; Phythian-Adams's tentative statement towards a 'rethinking' of local history has been conspicuous in its relative isolation.[1] While this short book is meant to raise questions for debate, it is not only in exchanges over the nature, aims and purposes of local history that a healthier state of affairs can be achieved. It is at the local and regional levels that fragmentation can be avoided, and synthesis of historical material and themes can be brought about. A critical survey of received frameworks can suggest where such synthesis may most easily be effective.

A germane example comes to mind. Probably no specialist body has done more to provide currently relevant framework material for many scores of local students than the Local Population Studies Society, with its emphasis on the teasing out of demographic statistics for parishes and localities. But a leading researcher and organizer in the Society, Dr Mills, has evidently concluded that narrow specialization of the demographic kind has gone too far for too long, and he has urged fellow-students to

> cover a wide range of topics in historical demography, historical
> sociology and historical geography in a more co-ordinated way at

> the local scale. I would like us to consider using the term 'community history' to embrace this basic idea ... there is the *problem* of defining communities, including territorial and non-territorial definitions, and the wisdom or otherwise of seeing our problems in the context of arbitrarily defined administrative entities. Thus, for example, it is a familiar criticism of family reconstitution that it should not be limited to one set of parish registers ... [2]

Exactly. Pre-industrial and industrial populations alike are notoriously mobile, and teamwork is called for in tracing the migrants. However, going beyond such methodological challenges, one cannot profitably consider studying the history of a locality without examining all the influences, demographic, economic and social, that may have conditioned the lives of local populations. Dr Mills argues for the study of the local 'community', but also urges that we should define the latter both in social (non-territorial) terms and in administrative (or territorial) ones. He argues, further, for the bringing together of a group of specialist standpoints.

It is interesting to note that Dr Mills in effect raises the problem of territory, or space. Most of his colleagues seem to have taken the parish for granted as a social entity, even though it is also a territorial unit, and yet is often seen as a 'community'. Some of this ground was surveyed in Chapter 4.[3]

All historians, including those denominated local, are concerned with events in space, or in given areas. It is the local historian who is most concerned with the spatial, because his or her territory is sharply defined or restricted, but that of the historian working at the county, national or even the European level is also quite clearly defined for many purposes. What is more, each type of historian is not only concerned with space, but with places, areas of which human beings are made conscious during long-term processes of living and lived experience. Generally speaking, historians do not regularly discuss the concepts of space or of place, which are taken for granted, and only localists may very occasionally be prone to run into these concepts. To many such historians, the latter will seem to be irrelevant to the challenges of fact-gathering and story-telling.

When an extent of human-occupied space is designated, it is used as a measuring instrument by historians in order to effect comparisons through time and, in practice, numerous assumptions about families, institutions, societies and other groups within the space are habitually made by the measurers. Space, seen in terms of superficial area, is often used to gauge apparent economic, demographic, administrative or social change within periods. Space is also used to *give an impression of the scale of human activity*, so that a project pursued in a small area will often be seen as micro-history, or as merely local instead of regional or national. The adjective 'local' of course implies 'small-scale', although the historical project concerned may in fact be a very elaborate study of human interrelationships, pursued in a concentration of detail that simply could not be applied to a larger area. In a case of this kind, the reader or student is in effect invited to think by analogy, and to imagine that he or she is looking, as through a microscope, at a small sample of tissue (or a drop of blood) taken from the much greater mass of a human body.

If the scale is somewhat altered, and the investigator looks at a small town and its hinterland, he or she will find himself or herself facing an *embarras de richesse* of detail, and will furthermore discover that space has another use or significance, in that it provides a series of linear or other measures of distances between points, as showing the likely movements of people or goods, or the difficulty or frequency of contacts between human beings, or simply the geographical locations of institutions, traders or festivals. If the investigator widens his or her focus to take in a still larger territory, he or she will risk perpetrating the ecological fallacy in tracing the locations of major political movements or events, or will map dialect terms or cultural usages, or will portray the sites of industrial developments. However, the key word here is 'map', because a map is an abstraction from as well as a representation of space, and in only a very few instances does the historian *experience* space as the man-or-woman-in-the-past experienced it. (Indeed, it was W.G. Hoskins's achievement to encourage the study of history 'on the ground', not merely in pursuit of archaeological traces but through following the work-routes of the peasant.) This is regrettable, because an actual walk along a market route or drove road would give the historian a sense of the limitations of the human condition that he or she sometimes sorely lacks.

This brings us to another function of the use of space in history (or in representations of history!), namely that of providing a pattern or grid for the measurement of adjoining territories, in order that certain kinds of interlocal or interregional comparison can be made. Here, it must be said, historians take the easy way out by using established administrative areas (parishes, hundreds, boroughs, counties) and their boundaries – census and other figures are aggregated on the basis of these official areas, and so it is tempting to make convenient comparisons of one parish with another, whilst sometimes forgetting to take actual areas into account. Other, and more serious, conundrums face the urban historian, who will find that population figures for a town, given from the earliest stages of its growth, provide an impressive-seeming index to its development. But the town boundary will have expanded several times and, in any case, relative densities of population should be shown, as well as the spatial measurements of the newly expanding areas. (Sadly, such refinements are rarely directly available from official statistics.)

Even in matters of modern political history, there are few cases in which space is wholly irrelevant. Particular movements are related to given spaces and places, often through proximity to centres of power and influence, and in order to seek for the origins and springs of a movement, it is necessary to search into the social history of a locality.[4] Of course, the language and terms of reference of a movement will be local in a few cases only, and will relate to a regional or a national political culture. Here we encounter the *centre–periphery* relationship, whereby a major centre of influence, usually the metropolis, is said ultimately to lead, guide or control the peripheral territories – often distant provinces or localities – through the circumstance that the apparatus and executive powers of government reside permanently at the centre. The assumptions of the latter are a received part of national culture.

This apparent exercise of power produces the effect of subordination, and the locality is then assumed to be with little proactive influence. We have to ask, meanwhile, whether space plays any significant part in power relationships of this kind, and the answer seems to be that modes of communication, which alter the effects of space or distance, most certainly do play such a part. However, the effects of space and distance are variable in history and a large manor near London, the Royal Manor of Havering, which has been the subject of an unusually intensive study by McIntosh, carried on its affairs between 1200 and 1500 with remarkably little official interference from the nearby capital.[5] In this instance, spatial position *vis-à-vis* the metropolis may be said to have been a negligible factor. Likewise, we may suspect that individual towns and villages throughout Britain were often, in medieval conditions and for practical daily purposes, far removed from direct power relationships wielded by government, the Church or distant overlords.

In these cases, place could presumably have a very special meaning to inhabitants, just as the word 'community' can doubtless have fitting applications to such villages or towns. Place, then, is not simply a matter of space (or a fortuitously chosen extent of territory). Like distance, which has been mentioned, place is a matter of human perception and recognition. Let us consider the views of social scientists regarding it, and then let us examine the problems of the concept of place in the historical context.

The greatest of these problems has lain in the impact of social change, over long periods, on place itself. Settlement in space has followed elaborate patterns of distribution dictated by the social division of labour under industrialism, and many different kinds of labour, occupation and group now occupy both space and place. This has meant, unsurprisingly, that the idea and concept of 'community' has itself been under stress, in that community is much less plausibly coincident with place, especially in the conditions of modern urbanization. 'Place' nevertheless obtains as a useful if rather elastic concept, and the local historian is doing nothing if he or she is not writing about it.

Both practically and philosophically, place is assuredly not the fixed entity that most local historians think it is. To innumerable students, local history is about a fixed place with a recognized and a usually fixed place-name and, indeed, some expert or experienced writers go to considerable trouble to uphold the myth of objective fixity. Hence, as we have noted (see Chapter 4[6]), Lewis has claimed that 'most local historians interested in a particular place do not have any difficulty at all … a group of small settlements served by a parish church normally bears a single name which expresses its unity and its identity as a community … '.[7] Leaving aside the questions of the impact of such events as the abandonment of hamlets and villages, population shift, the Black Death, ecclesiastical rearrangement, the rise of religious dissent, industrial settlement and town growth, neither space nor the application of the name itself is invariable. When a village becomes a town, and absorbs other villages, then perceptions of the significance of the place and its name alter. More than this, earlier perceptions of place and name have almost certainly altered over time, as groups of human beings within the locality have had different experiences and displayed changing attitudes to the place concerned.

Clearly the concept of place is important in this discussion. Of what does the concept itself consist? Here we must commence with a negative assertion: because the significance to contemporaries of a given place alters over time (and especially in recent times), then the place itself cannot be seen as simply contained within fixed administrative boundaries. If we come to examine the idea of a sense of place, which is a set of subjective views of place derived from residence within it, and from life experiences within its settlements and institutions, then it is unlikely that these views will pay much attention to boundaries. In any case, attitudes to place, elicited in the first instance through the practice and application of oral history, are so crucially important as to be the main concern of any local historian, and one would have thought that this – not some idealized notion of 'community' – was the first and most basic theme of the local historian, one which is uniquely distinguished from the pursuit and themes of any other branch of history. (The late Raymond Williams has also written about 'the structure of feeling' without reference to defined space, but in relation to lived, recorded and 'selective' culture.[8] But, where there is no reference to highly specific groups and situations, this concept is very difficult to pin down. It is not denied that such structures exist in large urban or regional areas, and the different manifestations of culture will help to condition attitudes to place.)

The sense of place, which is variable and frequently recurrent is, then, one aspect of the general concept of place. Social scientists have introduced refinements, and one of them, Giddens, has conceived the associated idea of the *locale*, the 'setting for everyday routines' and for social action.[9] This concept has also been condemned as 'nebulous', in this instance in a critical article by Duncan and Savage,[10] evidently because it refers to routines without specifying the uses of local resources that give rise to them, and also because it is vague in its general applications. However, the basic idea of the *locale* or setting is useful. It can be applied, for example, to a small town and its immediate hinterland, or to a small industrial district with a group of interlinked and common occupations in which the inhabitants follow similar or comparable daily or weekly paths. If we go back into more distant history, the concept of *locale* stands as a convenient reminder that the routines of local people do not necessarily adhere to this or that boundary – the historian will therefore look for evidence of actual regular movements and mental maps, and will not assume that those movements of people stay invariably within the parish or town.

The conceptualizers of place have added a further aspect of the latter for consideration, that of *location*. It may be that the actual location (or position) of a place will determine the degree and nature of the impact of its broader social context, but there is also a sense in which location relates to the geographical area 'encompassing the settings for social interaction as defined by social and economic processes operating on a wider scale'.[11] Location is important in the study of the interactions between places.

These three elements – the sense of place, locale and location – are relevant in the study of place in recent or in more distant history. The fact remains that these sociological and geographical concepts have not been readily adopted by historians, perhaps because they seem to point to some almost insoluble methodological problems. The sense of place is something which may appear in a recent or a still unfolding life history, and in the consciousness of human beings who are still with us, but evidence bearing on it from more distant history may be exceedingly hard to find. As has been pointed out, oral history can yield a great deal of information on a theme of this kind, but here another type of problem besets us, the so-called 'devaluation of place' described in detail by Agnew.[12] This devaluation, attributed to population mobility,

urbanization, rapid transport, the weakening of community values, nationalism, and the 'commodification' of people, places, land and labour, is held to have rendered the idea of place far less significant than it might otherwise have been. Agnew himself does not accept this sweeping characterization,[13] and points out that place has been confused with community, especially by political sociologists, and argues that the concept and reality of place are important to the study of society and the study of politics.

The fact is that the local historian is still likely to experience difficulty with the concept of place, especially in the light of current attitudes to this form of study. The geographer Paasi, for example, tells us, in contradiction to most British local historical assumptions, that, first, place is not 'an objectified everyday environment of individuals', nor is it 'an administrative frame'.[14] This theorist argues furthermore that 'place is not reducible to a specific locality, "site" or scale, or specific attitudes connected with these (physical or built-up environment, culture, social relations)'.[15] To summarize the drift of his (post-structuralist) argument, Paasi sees place as 'composed of situated episodes of life history', in other words, as entirely made of human experiences shared 'intersubjectively'.

Now, it is perfectly plain that a local historian working amid documents will apparently find little assistance here. The real message is surely fundamental: the ultimate subjects of local history are interacting groups of people, and to that extent it is wrong to write about place as a fixed entity, with a long-term or permanent administrative and geographical framework. It should be added that local history written in terms of 'landscape history', or of a fixed area to which document-based narratives are related, will inevitably fall into this error, as will any traditional semi-antiquarian approach which sees institutions and buildings as more significant than human beings or than the interactions of individuals or social groups. It remains to add that Agnew has argued that 'place is central to the structuration of society',[16] and it has a wide practical significance also. As the same writer has maintained, one can also conceive of 'a region of places',[17] and place can lie at the base of the concept of the region.

Before we move on to a consideration of the idea of the region, it will be as well to deal briefly with the common confusion of community and place, a confusion which belongs to the older, local historical tradition sufficiently criticized in these pages. It is easy to see where this confusion originates: 'community' is often used as a synonym for 'locality', as in phrases such as 'community school' or 'community centre'. But there is a long-established historical connection between the local community and landownership: as König remarked in his classic study *The Com-*

munity, the word *Gemeinde*, meaning the local community, in medieval times referred to the totality of inhabitants owning equal rights to land. That meaning has now changed, and a present-day translation of *Gemeinde* would give the usage as equivalent to the English parish or small local authority, and 'community' in that sense only. In the medieval usage, inhabitants were tied to location by the fact of landownership,[18] and 'community' could fairly be linked with residence and ownership in a given place. These links remained until recent times through land occupation rather than landownership, and the classic village community of the local historian is an agrarian as well as a rural one. This view of 'community' has all too clearly become a stereotype without real value, and an obstruction to the understanding and interpretation of modern societies. There are undoubtedly many relevant uses of the word 'community', just as there are clearly many types of community in modern urban and industrial conditions,[19] but they do not have to be based upon dynasties of land-occupiers or local inhabitants, nor need they be unbreakably tied to a given place.

The idea that large groups of people experience extra-local as well as local ties necessarily leads one to look for a theatre of activities which comprehends more-than-place or more-than-neighbourhood, but which at the same time partakes of the character of the places within it. It will be seen that a place and its life and routines are powerfully influenced, if not totally dominated, by the social and cultural trends and the institutions of a much wider territory. Not only do the inhabitants of a modern place have all manner of ties with this wider territory, they may have resided or worked throughout the latter. It should be said in fairness that many local historians are aware of such linkages, but that they find it convenient to treat the administrative county as the equivalent of a 'region'. However, the county, with its clearcut and long-established boundaries which will take little account of modern social and demographic movements,[20] may be a useful approximation to a region only if it surrounds given places to a considerable geographical depth – even then, its actual territory may be inconveniently limiting to the student of social and cultural movements.

These considerations are important, because – as Paasi has usefully asserted – a region is not an administrative unit, but a socio-spatial unit.[21] It is true that the tiers of administrative institutions in a region may help to consolidate it socially and even culturally, but centres of power and influence are not administrative alone, nor does the official wielding of power continually influence the life histories of most of the region's citizens. (Here is another reason for rejecting traditional county-type histories.) In other words, a region cannot be defined satisfactorily in terms of politics and the short-term exercise of power, for both are controlled by changing and sometimes transient groups, but political events and choices can be partially explained through analysis of regional or local social and economic factors, as Pelling and numerous others have tried to do.[22] This simple but incontestable fact explains the unsatisfactory outcome of the seventeenth-century 'county community' and Civil War debate, which seems (temporarily) to have foundered in the recognition that a county – such as, for example, Warwickshire – can have too many more or less coherent areas of social and economic distinctiveness within it to be fully useful as a period-framework for larger-scale political events studied at county level.[23] This consideration suggests that a 'region' (and Paasi does not give concrete examples for Britain) may be larger or smaller than a county in British terms, but that it may be partially defined in terms of shire-type or more general and cultural institutions. Here a great many factors come into play: geographical shape and definition, the homogeneity of areas in social and economic terms, socially and economically distinctive growth-patterns, the rural *and* industrial cultures within the region, and concentrations of given types of settlement, not to mention the institutions, networks and routes of communication (of information, ideas and commodities) within regional territory.

An example of the absorption of county-type institutions into a broader region may be seen in the so-called Lake Counties,[24] which have within their territory two distinct but related counties (Cumberland and Westmorland) linked over many centuries by a common rural peasant culture based on sheep-farming, a broadly common dialect and highly self-conscious speech-tradition, an educational tradition not unlike that of Scotland, common types of recreation (wrestling, hunting on foot, hound-trailing, dancing), a more recent, partly externally fomented symbolism of scenic splendour incorporating the Wordsworthian influence and, as a form of environmental base, a solid land mass or massif incorporating the northernmost part of Lancashire, which has also shared in the rural culture. To this general body of cultural institutions we can add: a limited but genuine military tradition represented by the joint county militia, the Cumberland and Westmorland Yeomanry and later the Border Regiment (which serves as a body related to the two main counties), with some First World War troop-raising pursued by the 'Yellow' Earl of Lonsdale; a regional antiquarian society embracing all three Lake Counties; some regionalism in the local press (for example, the *Cumberland and Westmorland Herald*, based in Penrith); and a tradition of locally patriotic societies based in London in the last century and designed to protect the interests of out-migrants in the metropolis.[25] By the second half of the last century, there was a great population shift to the west of the region, with the appearance of the industrial sub-regions of West Cumberland and Furness, and a new, polyglot industrial culture appeared, to absorb much of the original rural culture into its ways of life, including some of the institutions, symbols and myths described. The ensuing de-industrialization has not destroyed these institutions, but has transmogrified them to some degree.

Paasi, drawing on the original work of Karl Mannheim,[26] has pointed to the importance of his concept of *generation* in looking at the history of a region, and this idea, generation, is immensely important to the present discussion, because it mediates between place, with its individual life histories and experiences, and the large-scale, relatively enduring social history of the region itself. In the foregoing sketch of the history of the Lake Counties, covering (let us say) 200 to 300 years, the experiences of seven, eight or nine generations can be seen unfolding, each representing a collectivity of tens of thousands of individuals, and each encountering *structures of expectations*, 'based on the historical accumulation of experiences during the institutionalization of a region'.[27] These structures, argues Paasi, 'form a frame that is bound to a specific region, (one that is) quite permanent'. The structures can draw on outside influences, as well as on 'practices originating from the region itself', and this writer gives as an example external, non-locally controlled institutions such as the education system – perhaps not a valid example if we are considering the eighteenth century, but certainly true in the twentieth. This, as may be made clearer, is also of great importance in the argument, for regions are subject to broader, national cultural and administrative controls, imposed on the people of the region and sometimes at variance with their direct life experience – and there is a sense in which would-be standardization is of great importance to the historian, in that he or she can detect and even measure interregional variations at work. Generation is here seen as a specifically regional and local factor, one not more important than class, religion and gender, but crucial not only in reproduction of ideas, attitudes and the ways in which people use their knowledge of the world, but also in creating pressures for change as new cohorts make fresh contact with the regional socio-cultural system. In the process of socialization, this contact 'is never perfectly reproductive of tradition and modal personality'.[28] In other words, the idea of generation comprehends both continuity and change, but change always wins.

Generation does not express itself in regional consciousness only, for it can be local and national too, but it represents an awareness of belonging to a particular group, and also a consciousness of undergoing similar life experiences and sharing similar problems. This consciousness is enhanced, and is most sharply formed, in an approximate age-

range of 18–26 years,[29] when significant or formative events and attitudes will be most keenly registered. It should be made clear that the
latter can be shared across a region by members of the same generation,
without any necessity for direct physical contact – we are not discussing
a 'community' – just as persons can be conscious of belonging to a class
without such direct contact. Such sharing is strengthened when a keen
sense of place (or region) is present, and where relevant ideas, myths
and symbols are fostered or promulgated through institutions such as
the newspaper press, popular literature, political parties, churches and
some aspects of the education system. It goes without saying that speech,
dialect and language generally play a large part in fostering both regional and generational consciousness. In so far as the direct experiences of the individual's history within a locality or region are, through
collective or social life, crucial in helping to form the ultimate attitudes
of a generational group (the 'practical consciousness' of Marx and
Engels),[30] so too it must be remembered that 'official consciousness', a
conventional, national-cultural or standardized notion of events, will be
channelled to the people of a region through some of the agencies listed.

The social and cultural institutions here depicted, and the concepts
here briefly described, may together be plausible enough. The student of
regional history and social development is keenly conscious of the
difficulty of ascertaining generational attitudes to the region itself, and
to particular events. Yet it remains true that the unique function of
regional, as of local history, is more than demonstrating the interaction
of individuals and groups. Its ultimate purposes must be those of tracing the sentiments and long-term cultural attitudes which motivated or
even 'determined' the course of those interactions, and of discovering
manifestations of the sense of place. In other words, we take localism
and regionalism for granted, whilst remaining almost totally ignorant
of those mental sets which have lain at the foundations of both. The
historical growth of regional consciousness within many parts of Britain remains almost unexplored.

Hitherto, regional history has been interpreted within the terms,
concepts and limits of language of the national form of history, and has
been used as a proving ground for testing more general theories of
economic history and social and political development.[31] It is true, of
course, that the received historical frameworks for the study of regions
have benefited very considerably from these attentions, but the integra-
tion and synthesis of historical approaches and disciplines has most
emphatically not gained, and there have been few profitable and developing debates. Even the local historical demographers, the subjects of
Dr Mills's concern earlier quoted, have tended to concentrate on techni-
calities.[32] Unfortunately, too, current historical specialisms, and the

fragmentations of approach that they engender, have meant that there have been few successful attempts to look at regions holistically, and the most notable, executed over two generations, have in the main rested on a foundation of conventional county economic history or period politics.[33] Specialized papers, which are now numerous,[34] nearly always work within the fixed geographical frames of the county, diocese or borough, and hardly touch the subject of the socio-cultural region. Accordingly, there is little manifest concern for the historical develop-ment of regional consciousness as a theme.

It is true that the positing of the advantages of a 'holistic' approach raises problems, which may or may not be taken very seriously, of philosophy and methodology.[35] The most keenly felt sense of place is in the main local, not regional, but this does not mean that the region does not have a very real symbolic – or generational – significance to the member of a territorial regiment following the grim destiny of wartime, or that the name 'Highland' or 'Tyneside' or 'Black Country' does not have a resonance that dissolves county boundaries.

Meanwhile, it is also abundantly clear that the local sense of place, and the operative and changing locale, call for much more examination, and that local and urban social history must provide a foundation for the more advantageous study of the region in history, pursuing major themes rather than the heavy documentation and detail-for-its-own-sake which has hindered clarity of discussion. These studies must com-mence at a leaping-off point from the world as we now see it and probe back into history, asking questions on the way – the forward-approach from a vastly different world is simply an unprofitable and built-in convention which often starts with the wrong assumptions, including that which casts the tutor as God, when he or she should be questioning our immediate forbears.

The educational and self-educational implications for local history of this heterodox but necessary exploration are pursued in the final chapter.

Notes

1. Phythian-Adams (1987), *Rethinking Local History*, Department of Eng-lish Local History Occasional Paper, No. 1, Leicester University Press: Leicester, *passim*. The problems of regional history have often been touched upon in the *Journal of Regional and Local Studies*, but any conflict of ideas has been slow to develop. See, however, the report on the Nuffield supported conference (1990), 'Are British Regions Neglected?', *Journal of Regional and Local Studies*, 10, (2), Winter, 1–58.
2. Mills, D. (1993), Local Population Studies Society *Newsletter*, (10), Janu-ary.

3. See pp. 69–76 above

4. Cf. Pelling, H. (1967), *The Social Geography of British Elections, 1885–1910*, Macmillan: London and New York, *passim*, for an example well known to historians, many of whom have related local factors to politics. The importance and singularity of Pelling's work lay in the fact that he undertook a nation-wide comparative project, one which should provide local frameworks as starting points for future endeavours.

5. McIntosh, M.K. (1986), *Autonomy and Community: The Royal Manor of Havering, 1200–1500*, Cambridge University Press: Cambridge, *passim*.

6. See p. 71 above

7. Lewis, C. (1989), *Particular Places: An Introduction to English Local History*, London Library: London, 22–3.

8. *Vide* Williams, R. (1961), *The Long Revolution*, Chatto and Windus: London, 48–53, for a discussion of the 'structure of feeling'; for a more literary interpretation, *idem* (1973) *The Country and the City*, Chatto and Windus: London, 213, 298.

9. Giddens, A. (1981), *A Contemporary Critique of Historical Materialism: Vol. 1, Power, Property and the State*, Macmillan: London, pp. 29–41.

10. Duncan, S.S. and Savage, M. (1989), 'Space, Scale and Locality', *Antipode*, **21**, (3), 189.

11. Cf. Agnew, J.A. (1987) *Place and Politics: The Geographical Mediation of State and Society*, Allen and Unwin: Boston, 5–6; Paasi, A. (1991), 'Deconstructing Regions: Notes on the Scale of Spatial Life', *Environment and Planning*, **23**, (2), February, 248

12. Agnew (1987), ch. 5, 62–78.

13. Agnew (1987), 68–79 and *passim*.

14. Paasi (1991), 248.

15. Ibid.

16. Agnew (1987), 31.

17. Agnew (1987), 28.

18. König, R. (1968), *The Community*, Routledge: London, pp. 14–18; see also Plant, R. (1974), *Community and Ideology*, London, 38–9.

19. For differing approaches to modern urban and other 'communities', see again Frankenberg, R. (1966), *Communities in Britain: Social Life in Town and Country*, Penguin: Harmondsworth.

20. Perhaps the most interesting case of a largely irrelevant-seeming boundary is that between Derbyshire and Nottinghamshire in the Erewash valley. This cuts through a coalfield, and has little or no discernible effect on modern population movements or local culture. The writer is a native of this area, and has not overlooked the possibility that his attitude to boundaries may have been conditioned by the influence of this countryside! For a detailed historical characterization of the area, see the essay by Mitson, A. in Phythian-Adams, C. (ed.) (1993a), *Societies, Culture and Kinship: Cultural Provinces and English Local History*, Leicester University Press: Leicester, 24–76.

21. Paasi (1991), 249.

22. Studies by political geographers are theoretically interesting but, somewhat strangely, very rarely historically or even analytically down-to-earth, as Pelling (1967) tried to be; cf. Burnett, A.D. and Taylor, P.J. (eds) (1981), *Political Studies from Spatial Perspectives: Anglo-American Es-*

says on Political Geography, Wiley: Chichester, New York, Brisbane, Toronto, a collection of research papers.

23. Cf. Hughes, A. (1982), 'Warwickshire on the Eve of the Civil War: A County Community?', *Midland History*, 7, 1; *idem* (1987) *Politics, Society and Civil War in Warwickshire, 1620–1660*, Cambridge University Press: Cambridge.

24. Marshall, J.D. and Walton, J.K. (1981), *The Lake Counties from 1830 to the Mid-Twentieth Century*, Manchester University Press: Manchester, especially the Preface, viii–xii.

25. Marshall, J.D. (1984), 'Cumberland and Westmorland Societies in London, 1734–1914', *Transactions of the Cumberland and Westmorland Antiquarian and Archaeological Society*, New Series, 84, 239–54.

26. Mannheim, K. (1952), 'The Problem of Generations' in P. Kecskemeti, (ed.) *Essays on the Sociology of Knowledge*, Routledge: London, 276–322. The remarkable argument by Mannheim (especially 286 ff) deals with many of the more obvious problems – the effects of class, location, multiplicity and types of experiences – which arise from the theory of generation.

27. Paasi (1991), 249.

28. Paasi (1991), 251.

29. Cf. Lambert, T.A. (1972), 'Generations and Change: Towards a Theory of Generations as a Force in Historical Process', *Youth and Society*, 4, 21–45.

30. Williams, R. (1977), *Marxism and Literature*, Oxford University Press: Oxford, 30–44, where Raymond Williams discusses the social role and evolution of language.

31. Cf. Marshall, J.D. (1992), 'Proving Ground or the Creation of Regional Identity? The Origins and Problems of Regional History in Britain', in P. Swan and D. Foster (eds) *Essays in Regional and Local History*, Hutton Press: Beverley, 1–26.

32. See, in this respect, successive volumes of *Local Population Studies* published after 1968.

33. A survey of the earlier contributors to regional *economic* history is given in the Marshall essay, cited in note 31 above. One major work not there noticed is Rowse, A.L. (1941), *Tudor Cornwall: Portrait of a Society*, Cape: London, which is essentially 'political' in approach, while it attempts at the same time to do justice to economic and social factors. A mass of regionally located history now appears in article form in the academic journals cited in this book, just as the approach is currently (and unsatisfactorily) semi-popularized through the Longman 'Regional History of England' series.

34. Analysis of the subject-matter of several hundred articles appearing in the journals *Northern, Southern* and *Midland History* since 1966, shows a strong bias towards politics (including religious politics) and administration, and an almost complete acceptance of administrative boundaries as a predominant view among academic historians.

35. Cf. Chisholm, M. (1975), *Human Geography: Evolution or Revolution?* Pelican: Harmondsworth, 33–6, which raises the problem of the limitations of the holistic standpoint *vis-à-vis* regions – namely, that a regional society in all its tantalizing complexity cannot easily be thought to exist objectively of the observer.

CHAPTER SEVEN

Some Propositions:
Local History and the Challenge
of Civic Obligation

The previous chapters have raised questions which some will see as unnecessary, if only for the reason that tutors and teachers feel their positions to be threatened by a complex of sinister forces bearing down on adult education and on internal academic work. The kind of (largely absent) debate suggested here may seem to be a luxury in such circumstances, when the main preoccupation of many teachers is simply that of the survival of the courses that they foster and of the livings that the latter provide. Criticize some of the assumptions behind and within the courses, and one is then offering hostages to unsympathetic colleagues and administrators – so the reasoning can all too easily go. It would be an unkind individual who did not admit that there was some justice in the reaction outlined.

Had there been genuine debate and bolder experiment in earlier years, then this tract would have been largely otiose. The reservations and criticisms here given would have had what amounts to a prophylactic effect, and would have stimulated the anti-bodies necessary for the protection of a flourishing growth of the subject. As matters stand, the state of popular local history (if not of its more sophisticated variants) gives real cause for worry, in that practitioners are all too inclined to risk embracing antiquarianism – or, to use current publicity jargon, Heritage – in order to survive through the insurance of an adequate inflow of student numbers. To this extent, the psychology of the market is the overruling factor. Nor are these powerful undertows restricted to external courses or to adult education; the pressures of publicity methods and approaches to the public are felt everywhere in Academe.

There is, moreover, a multiplicity of pressures which can only lead to the cheapening of academic life and a threat to the integrity of intellect which the academic community purports to defend. To buckle before these pressures can only create more trouble for a later period, and for that reason alone it is necessary to reiterate a number of basic propositions. This apart, any element of defensiveness on the part of practitioners is surely uncalled for. As will be represented here, local and regional history together constitute what is arguably the most important of history's sub-divisions, in their relevance to large sectors of local inter-est, in their inherent appeal to town organizations and broader societies and in their role as synthesizers of an increasingly fragmented historical universe. The earnest pursuit of semi-antiquarian amusement is, in the light of this vast potential, a mere false trail. The realization of this potential does, however, rest upon the perception that whilst the best historical standards do indeed derive from academic practice and pre-cept, and whilst those standards must be continually refreshed at the same source (and the best amateur historians must always revitalize themselves in the same manner), practitioners must be willing to carry on dialogues with groups in a much wider society, and must be willing to learn directly from vast reservoirs of human experience.

Let us then commence with a number of very basic propositions, *Local historians must always consciously resist antiquarianism*, be-cause they are painfully exposed to the deadening effects of the latter, and they must be keenly aware of the distraction and inertia associ-ated with archaeology at the local level (but *not* archaeology as his-tory, which is necessarily perfectly legitimate). The more popular forms of narrowly focused archaeology greatly add to the antiquarian incu-bus, and it is very important that the psychology of the latter is systematically studied, perhaps through the works and activities of an organization such as English Heritage. 'Resisting', of course, strikes a negative note, and good and dynamic teaching, which excites the intelligence, cuts through the antiquarian barrier, just as it can find the right vantage points of influence in official and money-providing or-ganizations. Let nobody underestimate the threats represented by this malady at the present time. Conferences and study groups should discuss and disseminate teaching techniques designed to combat anti-quarianism.

Such study groups should cut into new territory, and they will also profit greatly from reviews of the possible educational effects of local and regional historical studies, and of those effects inherent in the study and pursuit of history-in-general. In theory, good teaching in these fields should train the mind of the citizen in a manner seen in any good history teaching. Local history, however, has derived much of its aca-demic esteem, not to say popularity, from its special role in introducing students to documents at a relatively early stage and, at the rather more sophisticated level, in introducing them to research techniques in a narrow but intensively studied field. This has meant that students often lack the general background that can be essential to the formation of certain kinds of judgement, and as a result *document-centred* teaching can be criticized, not only because students have to restrict their judge-ments, but because excessive concern with documents can lead to the nourishment of semi-hidden antiquarian leanings. This point, of course, was made earlier.[1]

It follows generally that *history teaching in this sphere must be concerned actively and explicitly with ideas.* These ideas must relate to a world which students find familiar, and must draw on their own great stocks of life experience. Some ideas, it is true, emerge from research methodologies and have attractiveness because they have the imprint of academic respectability, similar to some of those which historical demography makes available to students. The latter, however, must learn to ask their own questions and must apply their undoubted intelligences to social problems and movements which are much more general and which call for a less convergent approach – and for more open-ended answers as well as questions. Part of the reason for the popularity of document-centred training is that it deals with highly specific situations and is psychologically convergent. It is possible to master a situation or technique on a narrow front. On the other hand, adult students are often very uncomfortable with uncertain or incomplete answers and explanations, of the kind enforced by ongoing research, and much of this discomfort is attributable to lack of confidence and unfamiliarity with certain kinds of open-ended discussion. It remains true that it is good policy to distribute clearly marked and attainable tasks among the members of a group, for the reason already indicated. This approach does not, of course, preclude frequent discussion of ideas.

The importance of the latter cannot be understated. Ideas are the oxygen which gives life to otherwise inert material, and there can be no real growth in knowledge or enlargement of studies without them. Hence, *the idea of the received historical framework for a locality or region, to which allusion has been made,*[2] *in reality depends on constant debate and interchange,* and in a word on application of material to changing situations and for differing purposes. The piling up of a great system of factual references provides only the foundation of this reservoir of knowledge, which will remain a hunting ground for antiquarian collectors unless it is given form, direction and pattern by historical interpretations and by experimenters. It is true that certain systems of classification contain the germs (or dried seeds) of historical ideas, just as some accumulations of references reflect historical fashion during given phases as well as the dominant ideas of a given period.

If ideas are not constantly discussed, including alternative explanations for seemingly straightforward historical problems, then mature students will fall into the assumption that historical writing and construction or creation rests on successions of ascertained and (if possible) immutable facts, which are accordingly the first concern of the investigator – especially in local history, which is also seen as primarily a matter of factual accumulation. Ideas, in this context, may be dismissed as 'speculation', whilst the kinds of facts that appear in statistics are seen as giving mathematical precision (another part-reason for the success of local historical demography). Statistics, on the other hand, do appear to give control of the elusive and difficult to conceive, and they can be used to widen conceptualization in many scores of different ways. It is the exaggerated respect for the fact-in-isolation that marks a regression to antiquarianism.

Meanwhile, one of the great advantages of the well-organized and well-indexed received historical framework is that it reduces the labour of searching and seeking that has dominated so much of local history in the past, especially the leisure-time variety. To many hundreds of students, the act of searching for facts *was* the pursuit and practice of history, which was seen as a form of higher detective work. The implied excitement is not to be disparaged, and it can be memorable in the sense that childhood is memorable, but difficulty of collection makes mundane items seem much more important than they really are, and the business of history is interpretation and argument, not mere assembly. This essential impediment for beginners has been sentimentalized greatly, and is still regarded indulgently. The skill and facility of rapid access to relevant facts is an essential early constituent of training, even though the measurement of relevance is a knack that is acquired with greater difficulty.

Finally, the local historical world is still in an eotechnic stage in that the organizers of library facilities, the latter often excellent, still do not comprehend the possibilities of truly highly tuned historical organization. Librarians and historians remain separated by a professional divide, and fully resourced regional studies centres, an absolute necessity, are still in the future, just as the oxygen of ideas and debate is still to be made available in adequate quantity. The need for territorial and regional frameworks has a further importance and urgency which will commend itself to any person who has organized a course of regional or historical study.[3] It will be enough to observe that local history cannot develop without context, implicit or explicit, and for the most part that context has to be discussed quite clearly and explicitly.

We now come to the issue of *fragmentation*, which was discussed in Chapter 2, and to the related topic of *synthesis*, which is an ever-growing problem and challenge. The real or apparent seriousness of these topics is necessarily affected by standpoint. Hence, historians who see events and movements set out on a large scale over long periods may not at the same time see the increasing sub-divisions of history as offering any major problem. After all, it can reasonably appear to be true that multiplying specialisms are merely adding their own small shafts of insight to the general case, like the myriads of stars which are increasingly visible to ever-stronger telescopes. The local historian, however, does not have a macrocosm – or a universe – to play with. He or she has only a microcosm and, until a future dispensation provides the local historian with elaborate back-up resources, he or she has in the main, as far as primary information goes, only the somewhat standard-ized sources of the local and county records with which to work. Now, it is true that new specialisms and sub-specialisms give him or her what appear to be new resources, sometimes of a rich and exciting kind. These hopes, however, can be too easily disappointed. What is invigor-ating and significant to a scholar dealing with a general theme may provide only a footnote for the localist, and may even clutter up his or her more general discussions. Meanwhile, it is indisputably true that the work of synthesis, which rests on the pursuit of main or major themes, is rendered greatly more difficult by the importation of topics which owe much of their importance not to palpable historical relevance but to the accident of the development of new and specialized research techniques. This damping thought is too easily followed by another even more uncomfortable one: the parish or small locality is too small a unit for many aggregations of social, economic or demographic statis-tics, and we are once more back to the importance of the regional framework.

One must bear in mind, too, that local and even regional historical interpretations are part conditioned by the availability or non-availabil-ity of sources for given periods. Hence, the building of social structures is a laborious and frustrating activity for the early modern period, when whole populations are only laboriously kept under observation. The census schedules of the Victorian period, however, are apt to bulk very large in any serious local study, even where their use (to represent social structures) results in very little information or argument that is exciting or challenging. Where the student's approach is document-centred and specialism-centred, the literal meaning of fragmentation will be all too apparent in his or her work. Meanwhile, it should not be imagined that only the vulnerable amateur is threatened by fragmentation. The dis-ease can appear, in advanced form, in the work of professional histori-ans whose eyes are constantly on fashionable techniques or on sub-topics with some weight in national history, and whose work becomes sadly intractable as a consequence.

We now come to the vexed question of synthesis, the bringing to-gether of different types of case, argument – and, dare we say it, specialism – into a purposeful and systematic general discussion de-signed to answer a main question or a number of related questions. In the case of local or regional history, one might add 'in such a way as to throw light on an entire local society'. There is, of course, a philosophical and a psychological difficulty here, for an 'entire local society' is very difficult to comprehend in one relatively extensive inspection, let alone in an instant. Yet it must be regarded as an entity, and explored as a mass of interrelated groups, interests and associations.[4] During much of a town's or a locality's history, these interrelationships may be difficult to trace, but at times of crisis (depression and industrial failure, a strike, a cotton famine, or even a war) the linkages become much more evident. The investigator, meanwhile, must distinguish between long-term or cultural influences which come from the greater province or the nation at large, like many of the formative and guiding pressures of twentieth-century education, and those which are distinctively local. This will lead him or her to place the adverb *'where?'* in probing questions relating to the location of events within the areal or sub-regional framework; *'when?'*, the discussion of the timing of events, may then be followed by a *'why?'* question. There will be many sections of analysis, whereby the behaviour of an institution (a school board, a trade union, a local authority) is dissected, but the movement will be one directed towards a survey and illumination of the whole. Now, it has long been recognized that local and urban history can do this, but the significance of their synthesizing functions is rarely discussed, perhaps because the problems presented by fragmentation are equally ignored, and as a possible consequence innumerable studies fall prey to the latter to a greater or lesser degree.

Synthesis, in present circumstances, means rather more than looking at an evolving society holistically. It means making linkages between the main forms of or approaches to history, the social, the economic, the demographic, the agrarian, the religious, the political, the administrative, and so on. Such prescriptions can be challenging in the extreme, and a striking example comes to mind. The lack of contact between two sub-species of researcher/writer, namely business and labour historians, has been remarked upon.[5] Yet a collaboration between such historians could add significantly to the history of a locality, in that the history of industrial decision-making could be linked with the fate, organization and attitudes of a labour force which represented a significant proportion of the inhabitants. In practice, the localist or urbanist may be obliged to wear several disciplinary hats,[6] to the extent of covering all the historical sub-divisions outlined, an intensely educative process which can also be daunting. There are many illustrations of the types of linkage one can then make. The growth of a mid-Victorian industry brings in migrants from Ireland, who settle in a number of localities, and whose Catholicism conflicts with the views of the Protestant groups nearby. The social and domestic attitudes of the Irish have repercussions for local government at town and county level. Meanwhile, more general political movements in the area are affected by this conflict, which takes violent form as national politics, and like Fenianism, exacerbates feelings. Local education systems are put under strain, whilst fluctuations in the main or heavy industries affect labour forces, who, in the trough of a depression, create problems for charitable bodies and for the churches. In the somewhat longer term, the heavy industries create an appreciable number of casualties, and the inadequacy of hospital provision is made the subject of local agitation. A quick glance will show that every one of the now current historical sub-divisions is here covered or interlinked, except perhaps the 'agrarian' – and a closer examination of Irish immigrant behaviour would inevitably bring that division into the net.

This conspectus has the virtue that it demonstrates the interconnections between sub-regional movements, but it is only a necessary matrix, and the significant or intensely shared political and social experiences usually belong to much smaller groups, such as the Irish Catholics and Protestants who have been in conflict in particular localities. The full story of the latter could not be explored without the general background or context which, in so far as it is fully known and understood, may give a series of keys to motivating forces in society. Deciding on the most powerful of these is a major responsibility which the historian must carry.

So far the discussion has touched upon this or that locality in a wider context. *Local history cannot be adequately written without this context.* However, Chapter 6 explored some of the problems associated with the concept of place, and use of this word has so far been eschewed. In the territory given as an example, the extractive industries have been responsible for the planting of a series of new settlements, which have in turn produced new awarenesses of place within and round the parishes in which the settlements have appeared. These awarenesses are very real, and they are only partially connected with any sense of community in the same places – there are several discernible 'communities' in the places mentioned. The evolution of these places has to be examined in the wider and sub-regional context, and degrees of awareness are only incidentally manifested – the immigrant Irish, for example, take little part in town or local government, and they keep strictly to their own ethnically related organizations. In the following generation, the sub-regional trade union movement breaks down this exclusive attitude to some degree, and the Irish become more readily assimilated.

In other localities, meanwhile, long-established awarenesses of place remain, strengthened by patterns of work, routine and movement which change only slowly. Yet, underneath this apparently largely local valuation given to place, many hundreds of people emigrate to the USA and the former British colonies (South Africa draws many miners whose work has failed in this British area). Emigration can be examined in several ways, and one interpretation of this drastic and desperate measure is that it embodies a more or less total rejection of place – or, just as appositely, a sense that the place, with its association with kin and with a way of life, has rejected the out-migrant. (Work has in any case moved out of the narrow locality into the wider area, which is still a 'place' or home territory.) Groups of workers and their families go on to establish self-conscious settlements in the American West;[7] letters suggest that their awareness of the home place is carried with them, and part of the local history of the places concerned is sketched out within another continent, having moved far away from the original location. This kind of local history is very difficult to write, but it can be far more true to the experiences of human beings than is the formal exploration of institutions and events within an ecological framework and bounded territory that nowadays passes for such history. Meanwhile, only general context, which in this case has an international dimension, will tell us how awarenesses of place have changed.

It can be objected that these reservations and warnings relate only to the history of the recent industrial world, and that the life of the rural 'community' remains much the same through several centuries. Recent research into migration in early modern England[8] now demonstrates far more flux and movement than was thought likely only a few decades ago, and the single place is no longer a strictly suitable subject for prolonged attention. A parish which loses (let us say) a third of its people in a generation is hardly a self-reproducing entity in the strict sense, even though it may retain some family stocks for centuries.

The provision of regional historical context is a matter of public will and individual well-doing ; regrettably it cannot be performed by a few acts of private goodwill through a voluntary association, or through the library service, or through a university or college alone. Much can be done by regional research centres of the kind already established, but these can only help to point the way by providing studies of regions and by outlining research that needs to be pursued. Such centres need resources. Meanwhile, research on given local localities, towns or societies ('communities') cannot remain aloof from the people who are the subjects of study, but must be drawn comprehensively to their attention.

It is extraordinary that few persons have noticed the implications of this putative public involvement. In the first place, local history, properly researched and written, is in effect supplying members of a settled local public with the basic details of their own past, or that of their families. It should embody some of their crucial life experiences, and should further set out or explore some of the formative influences on their families and ancestors. Now, most of us gain a sense of identity from past life experiences and memories, which add another dimension to our personalities. Many human beings perforce have an uncertain sense of the more distant past, although it is significant that millions of them are drawn towards it nevertheless, and the intense interest shown in the recent past, especially by elderly citizens who are interviewed, suggests that there is a powerful latent involvement that is never fully engaged. Filling in significant details of past experiences, drawn from actual cases, is clearly a work of much importance to many hundreds of people. It is evidently the case that great numbers of citizens long for an adequate valuation and explanation of their past, and it is this sentiment that partially explains the striking popularity of family history. The past, to them, is to be explained in terms of family fortunes and movements, but these cannot themselves be given real point without a background study that is rarely present and which is only now seen as increasingly important.[9]

Further consideration can lead to an arresting conclusion. The act of organizing, writing and publishing a local history of a large population (and its antecedents) surely embodies an obligation to do justice to the people who are written about. The latter are not merely a group of subjects, or actors, about whom certain conclusions may be drawn, perhaps to be included in an article or occasional paper. They are human beings whose identities should ideally be enhanced by what is written about them, and whose history has the collective impact of many scores or hundreds of brief biographies. Hence, the local history of a town or district should have far more general significance than does the published biography of an individual,[10] however famous or talked-about the subject of the biography may be. It is true that the famous individual may be by definition unusual, whereas a description of the quotidian may seem to have little that is exceptional or exciting about it. Yet it is the accurate and sensitive probing of the quotidian that constitutes much of social history, and what is workaday to one population or constituency may be almost completely unknown to another. The more detailed and specific social morality of this obligation implies a respectful attitude to the achievements and obligations of labour, but this is no more than any democratic civil society might be expected to accept. Moreover, this is an attitude easily communicated by almost any major oral history project,[11] whereby it soon becomes evident that a man's or woman's past work (and occupation) is something far too serious for misrepresentation or joking.[12]

The older and established inhabitants are here given pride of place. The obligation to represent them adequately does not extend only to past daily work. The recording and accurate discussion of their life experiences implies just as much commitment to effective and respectful reproduction. In-migrants and younger groups indeed call for attention for specific purposes, and samplings of persons throughout such a social structure as has been identified are *de rigueur* – industrialists, councillors, administrators, and professional people. Meanwhile, sound oral history depends on the effective and corroborative use of printed and documentary records, and what takes shape here is a local history project of a rich and stimulating kind. The conduct of contemporary recordings by local history societies is an accepted activity, one advocated by the British Association for Local History, and all that is suggested here is an extension backwards in time, seeking the answers to certain basic questions. One of these putative questions is highly relevant to the argument in this book: What communities of interest and activity do local people see themselves as belonging to? These groupings would consist mainly of business, political, occupational and leisure-time 'communities'. The ensuing discussion, carried on through a specially arranged study group or team from a local history society, would have profound repercussions for any later or more conventional views of the local community, and problems of definition would by that time have had a thorough airing. Having identified some contemporary 'communities', the group could set itself the task of tracing their evolution in recent or more distant time – some specific industrial communities in the broader district or neighbourhood, some village-like communities in the urban setting, the local Chinatown or no-go area, and some socially distinctive suburban settlements. Councillors and local government officers could be shown to have their own areas of common interest and activity, and this brings us to the major question of communal involvement in the project itself.

It is clear that such a project as is here taking shape would not only need far more resources than an adult class or local history society commonly has available, it would represent the absolute antithesis of antiquarianism in its approaches, it would be participatory on a large scale and it would involve local authorities and voluntary associations throughout the area studied. This project would be of obvious interest to councillors and administrators, because it would trace the evolution of major movements and key events in local government, and it would represent nothing less than an examination of the working of local civil society. As such, it should attract resources from a group of agencies within that society. It would have to utilize and command a considerable academic input, but it would also reach out to schools and the local education system, and it would not be bound by the common academic constraints of specialist publication, supervision and attitude

– it would be public in the broadest sense, and would use publicity on a grand scale. The historian leaders or supervisors would also be public servants in the true sense.

In setting a fairly elaborate organization into being, the promoters would be able to do more than discharge their civic obligation. They would be able to call in resources provided by *civic group-esteem*, sometimes seen as civic pride. This, in the past, has called forth the 'booster' town histories to which Asa Briggs made memorable reference,[13] and the sentiment can be utilized positively, especially when it is understood that the clumsy or ill-presented tourist propaganda brochure carries little ultimate weight, and that a locality can be proud of altogether less ephemeral achievements. There is a qualification: the nature of civic pride can be explored by questioning local citizens, and the 'official consciousness' called forth when history is written by local government officers can soon be examined in an altogether different perspective. Citizens do have pride in their localities, but footballers may play a larger part in the formation of this pride than do councillors. The shortcoming of the booster history is that it attempts to create pride, instead of investigating it, and the problem of how far to go along that road is a major one. A town may be seen quite accurately as a product of the labours of its citizens, and as an elaborate outcome of the work of multiple groups but, if civic disasters (such as high-rise flats in the 1960s) are not coolly and carefully discussed, the project as a whole becomes suspect, and those concerned learn nothing.

Bear in mind, too, that most of the inhabitants will have had no part in municipal or industrial decision-making, and accordingly another of the major concerns of a civic project of this kind will be that of investigating and discussing the roots and processes of important local decisions. A well-conducted oral history sub-project will almost certainly elicit a great deal of information bearing on the history of such decisions and processes. It is, moreover, essential that the uses of power by responsible persons and groups are discussed alongside the more mundane recordings of work and quotidian life, for in this way a balance of standpoints is maintained. Sometimes the 'balance' within a topic may turn out to be a bizarre one; for example, a northern town that suffered from high unemployment between the wars managed to give hundreds of unemployed males work on the creation of public amenities such as a park and a coastal road.[14] More general prescriptions, such as a reasonable maintenance of balance as between political subjects and the effects of socially and economically relevant decisions, will become visibly important to the long-term working out of a project, whilst contributions from labour and business historians together can introduce an element of penetration that might otherwise be missing.

For the rest, choices of subject-matter may in the end prove to be almost limitless (although those which commend themselves urgently can also be quickly recognizable), and the acts of choice will take place only after much public discussion. After all, people often have a shrewd idea of the influences which have most affected their own lives and destinies, and in adding their weight to certain decisions, they will help this piece of history to take shape and to gain it recognition as belonging to the public domain. If, meanwhile, the organizers and their supporters could, at key stages in the working out of the project, dissolve conventional subject-divisions and review the entire history of the district at generation stages – bearing in mind Karl Mannheim's concept of generation[15] – then real strides towards the essential act of synthesis might be made. For to pause at the generation stages allows not only for synthesis, but for comparison and a determined attempt to measure the nature and character of social change.

In the intervening stages, conventional academic subject-divisions should be used as launch-pads only, and wherever possible, fairly large and sometimes open-ended questions should be posed. Hence, a general question designed to go to the heart of local educational history (covering in this instance no more than two or three generations), and meant to avoid the lengthy recitations of institutions which might more suitably find a home in the Victoria Histories or in a town index in the library, would be: 'What was taught in our schools, and what effects did it have?' Such a sub-project would not be easy to execute, because many educational historians find that conventional sources are unhelpful in answering such questions, and reliable measurements of effect are hard to formulate. Nevertheless, the co-operation of teachers and local authorities, and the use of oral commentary and reminiscence, could reveal important data at crucial stages, as could the comments of official statisticians, employers and educationalists. One has to bear in mind that twentieth-century education systems are conditioned by national cultural trends and attitudes, and local or provincial influences are very secondary. However, this reservation surely does not mean that local projects have nothing of interest to report, for the latter may, through enhanced representativeness, have much wider significance than the merely local. For example, a close study of the local or regional uses of literacy and, in particular, of those reading habits developed immediately after school, might tell us a great deal of the effects of education! (One wonders whether George Orwell really did say the last thing about boys' and girls' comics.) Processes of self-education should not escape attention and, where feasible, analysis, and minority concerns could be fairly included, but the popular view should receive unflinchingly fair treatment, the central purpose of the entire project being kept constantly in mind – namely, that of raising the historical consciousness of significant sections of an entire local and civil society. No matter that scores of respondents claim nostalgically that comics richly enhanced their lives; if this was indeed the case (and it probably was), then the presumed fact should go in the historical record.

Civic and public pride or esteem are made up of many particles of attitude and experience, and some of these particles relate to pride in a given school and its education, or in one of many scores of institutions. That many such attitudes are irrational is a consideration that historians and other professionals have to learn to face fearlessly. Hence, a school will attempt to build esteem for itself by advertising its most distinguished old boys or girls, as though these products fairly represented the bulk of its work, and the scope and range of what one may call 'large-scale public irrationality' must also be faced. Historians, sociologists and other academics seek rational explanations, and the world of myth, folklore and tradition is an especially frustrating one in which to organize part of a project. Its small band of practitioners have to content themselves, for much of the time, with recording and collecting,[16] and so they tend to drift into an antiquarian backwater, ignored by the great majority of professional historians.

Perhaps one of the greatest failures of local and regional history in this country has been that of failing to identify, and therefore to trace the history of, the nature of traditional images and stereotypes relating to institutions, counties and countrysides. Not only has the nature of civic pride and esteem gone partly unexplored, such history has had virtually nothing to say about local and related aspects of national patriotism. One of the main unifying themes and questions designed to bring together many historical strands, and therefore to achieve a necessary synthesis, is 'what has been the effect of two world wars on successive generations in X?', and of course the nature of local (and some aspects of national) patriotism deserves and requires exploration. Patriotism's manifestations have forms which are much more specific than might appear, and are traced in the histories of county and territorial regiments, often published as a form of displaced and heroic local history, whereby men from a town (such as Accrington) or a county (the Lancashire Fusiliers, the Border Regiment), in the course of recording terrible sacrifices, find men from the same town and countryside in the trenches of the Somme or Gallipoli, or facing panzer units in the fields of France.

These brave men often deserve to be rescued from the typical regimental history but, that obvious reservation apart, we have to face the novel secondary question, 'has place been devalued by war?' A little reflection may show that nothing of the kind has happened. The modern history of Accrington, for example, has acquired a major theme and tradition through its 'Pals' battalion, and the whole point of territorial regiments has been that they deployed the patriotic spirit of men from the same countrysides. Sometimes the perception of a countryside has been surprisingly accurate, and the Notts. and Derby Regiment, known as the Sherwood Foresters or Robin Hoods, has been based on the coalfield of a more or less homogeneous industrial region, in which the county boundary has not always had great significance.[17] The reference to Sherwood Forest is, of course, a calculated use of existing long-term tradition, at once romantic and mendacious, and at this point one has to ask how far traditions are manipulated or even invented, or prolonged by artifice. Hence the Derby County football team has the traditional name of the Rams, after a popular and recitational song, 'the Derby Ram', which is now all but forgotten or relegated to the occasional folk evening or recording.

It may be that many traditions have been resuscitated by journalists, and if this is so, research can sometimes reveal the process. Yet there is something beneath and beyond the fashions set going by the press, a deep desire to cling to tradition and to be part of a continuity, not because necessarily self-indulgent emotions are at work, but because the traditions help to form an identity. These emotions can be linked through not too many steps to the team patriotism of football crowds, expressed through the mass excitement of people who would otherwise have lives of little recognized meaning or esteem. As has been observed, civic pride and football prowess are not far separated.

These observations take one far into what could and should be the subject-matter of local history, which is not wholly that of a specialized anthropology. Comment on them cannot match the judgement of the expert anthropologist, but the local historian can fulfil a vital function by observing, collecting and analysing *attitudes and sentiments* as they appear in his historical sources. It is a sad observation that facts, to many hundreds of local historians, have meant events, or the details of institutions, and rarely or never have they signified expressed sentiments, attitudes or emotions. If the historian can show the exact circumstances in which the latter were uttered, so much the better. Nor is this merely a matter of public-spiritedness towards other historians; local history itself has to work hard to seek evidence of the *affective*, the world of sentiment. Local historical research has a vast amount to do in the field of the recording and measurement of linkage through presumed contact and proximity, even though the latter is an inadequate guide to 'community'.[18]

Here, then, we have three levels or types of involvement: the field of public and, where necessary, official participation; the investigation of civic esteem in its relationships to local civil society; and the search for the origins of specific kinds of local and other patriotism. These three kinds of involvement together make a powerful demand on historical responsibility, and there should be no possible doubt as to how great this charge is likely to be. The measure of the local historian's failure is to be found not in many perfectly defensible teaching activities which are currently pursued, but in the large-scale invasion of the historian's domain by officially supported 'heritage' and antiquarian activity, combined with a massive devaluation of the nature of local history itself. To blame amateur and leisure-time practitioners for this is to miss the point completely, for there is a substantial failure to perceive the nature of the problem on the part of academic historians. They are apt to feel that they have discharged a public duty when a capable graduate researcher has written a history of place X or town Y. The latter may or may not consult people in the locality concerned, and only in relatively few cases will the dissertation or thesis be published and publicly discussed, and, much worse, the study concerned will evoke little discussion in the years that follow. Eventually, many such works will accumulate in university libraries, some of them far out of range of the local historians in the areas written about. The only redeeming or hopeful feature of this state of affairs is that the spread of academic training courses will encourage members of local historical societies to make full use of the hundreds of such graduate works now available. The auguries are not wholly encouraging, because there is abundant evidence that academics themselves do not have time to use this great reservoir of research to strengthen the study of regional history,[19] and to support a debate that would bring such works into use.

Certain necessary resources are often wholly lacking, and there are, after all, few professionals in the field to undertake a vast operation and to discharge throughout Britain the major duty outlined. It need hardly be pointed out that the public project outlined in this chapter is a beguiling vision, one based, it is true, on many areas of existing practice and on a variety of encouraging individual experiences garnered over a lifetime. It is the type of major public project that could be entertained by a new university seeking to cement its relationships with a substantial cross-section of the people of a nearby town or district, and willing to invest more than nominal resources in a regional history centre – and also to second one or several members of staff to the project. This sounds so far removed from present probabilities as to be hardly worth further thought. Yet the vision has certain uses, and it conjures up no more in the way of bold and ambitious resource employment than the present uninspiring situation calls for. The local history campaigner who has no vision of this kind is probably very complacent about what he or she teaches and about what could be achieved in his or her working territory were a measure of real help forthcoming. That the project could have very considerable advantages for the university or college concerned (not all of them to be measured in pounds and pence) goes almost without saying, and its contribution to the enhancement of citizenship as well as to the understanding of history could be substantial.

Some loose ends remain. Teaching history retrogressively is a stratagem to be employed in certain circumstances and is not a proposed invariable rule. It enables the newcomer to history to proceed from the partially known to the mainly unknown, and the approach is especially suitable for groups of mature students commencing a serious study of local history. Nevertheless, the reason for the approach must be carefully explained, for most persons interested in local history see the latter as a form of chronicle moving forward through time, if possible from the Iron Age to the present, and they do not think of it as having bearing on recent civil society and on the latter's ideas and problems. There is nothing heterodox about such an idea; local history teaching is justified because it communicates the ideas and concerns of history teaching in general[20] (including those which provide a fine introduction to the study of past societies), and only secondarily because it provides a form of training in the use of original sources. But if the serious student of local history is to have an adequate grounding in more general historical study, and still derive the advantages of studying a locality with which he or she is familiar, then he or she must commence with a critical examination of a world to which he or she is accustomed. Indeed, it is difficult to guess what advantage he or she can derive from a superficial but locally related collection of facts about a vaguely perceived place in distant time, and it is significant that teachers of the subject have seized upon the more complex challenges offered by the study of, let us say, local historical demography in the early modern world, for the student does here encounter the idea of interpreting details of comparable local societies.

A more general study that *contrasted* medieval or early modern society with that of a more recent time and place would be a very valuable addition to local historical training in almost any context, and such an enterprise would be a valuable extension to the civic project already envisaged, as would specialized courses on certain periods. These would move both backwards and forwards in time, as analytical historical studies often do, and there would be no attempt to look at history retrospectively only. The student who labours with love, however, needs to be able to distinguish between the languages and symbols of different ages and times, and to have a general historical education based on comparisons and contrasts, and an ability to look round with a sense of direction in whatever world he or she finds him or herself. This attribute is ultimately far more important than a thorough knowledge of one period only.

A movement, an event or a process needs to be studied as each unfolds through time, and what is true about the individual event is also true about its developing background. History cannot be studied except (much of the time) forwards through its grain but, equally, a perplexing world or universe has to be brought under control, and a situation must be examined from every angle.

To return to the more specific aspects of a public project: in the earliest stages, these will not automatically appeal to the antiquarian sentiments which seem to condition much recruiting to local history courses at the present time, and the call should be to the somewhat different psychology surrounding family history – the skilful collection of names and relationships has here run its course in innumerable cases, and the students concerned wish to fill out their knowledge of work, occupations or local backgrounds. This will be a major preoccupation. Likewise, this part of the book has had little to say about the detailed organization of projects, mainly because primers purporting to teach local history have become numerous, and because it is the purpose of this text to discuss what such handbooks do *not* in general include.[21] So many dubious premises and assumptions are implicit in these guides that it has seemed to be a matter of importance to deal with a few of the most outstanding, in order that critical discussion can proceed, especially on training courses in local history. Accordingly, the writer has felt under no obligation to suggest more in the way of positive action than appears in this final chapter, after all, he is not responsible for the developments of the past 50 years, and was one of the very few to raise some difficult questions during that period.[22] If the reaction of teachers and instructors in local history is that the highest standards are maintained and that effective and insightful local histories – including those of towns – are regularly written *and* published by non-professionals, then there is nothing further to be said. If the same instructors are quite certain that a vast public does not deserve or need to be rescued from the most basic antiquarian misapprehensions (which miraculously disappear when members of the same public enrol in classes conducted by them, the instructors), then again there is no further rejoinder.

However, it may also be that there is abundant room for a little vision. It is a *non sequitur* that a threat to academic or teaching standards in one age must necessarily depress any standards of study, teaching or historical achievement in an age which follows, and it may be that the discouragements of the present century, and the disappointed ideals of pioneers of adult education, may yet be followed by further very real gains and new aspirations. The unparalleled growth of higher education in the 1960s was nevertheless accompanied by a no less remarkable achievement, the establishment of the Open University, which showed widespread longings for serious study and academic achievement among a largely new public. Perhaps, after all, such reservoirs of serious endeavour are still to be found in an age which has grown to value individual achievement but which has yet to gain mental health through social involvement and dedication. In matters of the history of the near at hand, a cheap and easy populism with a top-dressing of academic training may one day be followed by the development of a genuine people's history, and it has been a purpose of this chapter to suggest how the latter could be brought about.

Notes

1. See especially the discussion in Chapter 3, 52 ff.
2. See Chapter 5, 89–91.
3. The 'context' commonly chosen during the organization of pioneering courses in the 1960s and later was the administrative and historical county.
4. The psychological or philosophical difficulty of comprehending an entire region, in all its ramifications and linkages, is discussed briefly in Chisholm, M. (1975), *Human Geography: Evolution or Revolution?*, Pelican: Harmondsworth, 36.
5. This type of multi-disciplinary endeavour or enterprise has highly respectable antecedents in the British Association volumes produced by a succession of British universities, and purporting to deal with each university's region from the standpoints of a variety of disciplines. It is the synthesis of disciplines which has proved elusive.
6. Some themes in regional history lend themselves to a cross-disciplinary (or 'cross-conventional-topics') treatment. Hence, when migration from the Lake Counties is discussed, it can be seen to focus attention on housing shortages, the state of farming, manifestations of discontent, agrarian trade unionism, railway-building, employment patterns in the region itself, job aspirations, marriage patterns, illegitimacy, family structures, the trade cycle and depressions, overcrowding, sanitation, death rates and wage levels. Any one of these topics could demand specialist treatment at some time, even though the problems of fragmentation would then remain; in this instance all topics have been made relevant. Cf. Marshall, J.D. and Walton, J.K. (1981), *The Lake Counties from 1830 to the Mid-Twentieth Century*, Manchester University Press: Manchester, ch. 4.
7. Cf. Trescatheric, B. (1981), 'The Furness Colony: The History of an Emigration Society in Great Britain and Minnesota from 1872 to c.1882', M. Litt., University of Lancaster.
8. As shown by Clark, P. and Souden, D. (1988), *Migration in Early Modern*

England, Hutchinson: London, *passim*. See also Spufford, P. (1973, 1974), 'Population Mobility in Pre-Industrial England', *Genealogists' Magazine*, 17, (8), (9) and (10), December, March and June, 420, 475 and 537 respectively.

9. The numerous territorial family history societies now give increasing amounts of attention to background and social history which might be to the assistance and encouragement of members. For what are now representative views from the standpoint of a local history tutor, see Hey, D.G. (1986), *Family History and Local History in England*, Longman: London. This interesting and varied study does indeed give 'background'.

10. A corollary of the argument here put is that any work of local history implies real responsibility in treatment and approach, a point which local history societies could well notice.

11. Numerous such projects have been described and reported in the pages of the *Oral History Journal*.

12. This point was long ago established by the late George Ewart Evans, who was enabled, after many years of interviewing, to assert categorically that 'a man does not lie about his work'.

13. Briggs, A. (1962), *Victorian Cities*, Odhams: London, Introduction, 51–3.

14. The reference here is to Barrow-in-Furness, which in 1923–24 acquired a Public Park extension, two coast roads and other amenities as a result of the period indicated.

15. See Chapter 6, Note 26, in this volume.

16. It should be noticed that among the few bodies which organize systematic study of folklore and some traditions (for instance, the Folklore Society), the Centre for Cultural Tradition and Language at the University of Sheffield plays an important part in this field.

17. See Mitson, A. (1993), 'The Significance of Kinship Networks in the Seventeenth Century: South-West Nottinghamshire', in C. Phythian-Adams (ed.), *Societies, Culture and Kinship, 1580–1850: Cultural Provinces and English Local History*, Leicester University Press: Leicester, 24–76.

18. In a recent statement, Charles Phythian-Adams commences by deploring the preoccupation of local historians with 'place' as a given entity around which everything must be constructed. This is to be welcomed; likewise his plea that historians should pursue the histories of local societies through 'societal history' within regions and neighbourhoods is well worthy of furtherance, provided that there is not, as seems possible in this case, a regression to the ecological and geographically deterministic (as relating to *pays*, watersheds and drainage systems) as well as to a possible over-reliance on kin linkages as defining elements. The theory here is interesting but cloudy; methodology and definition deserve a more thorough discussion. Phythian-Adams, C. (1993b), 'Local History and Societal History', *Local Population Studies*, 51, Autumn, 30–45.

19. The evidence for this statement (that academics do not fully utilize the great volume of regional theses and dissertations, is to be found in the relative absence of references to such works in regional papers and articles. However, many historians supervise these works.

20. Books expounding the value and uses of history are numerous; the author has found such works stimulating, although the educational applications of this great subject are perhaps best dealt with in the journal *Teaching History*.

21. See the local history textbooks in the list given in Note 2 to Chapter 3 in this volume.
22. See Note 6 to Chapter 4 in this volume.

A Corrective to Enthusiasm: Raphael Samuel and the Popular Past

The percipient and lively comments of Raphael Samuel have been quoted at several points in this book, usually with approval if not with total agreement.

In the first volume of his study *Theatres of Memory, Vol. 1: Past and Present in Contemporary Culture*, Samuel (1994) demonstrates the width and variety of popular interest in the British past through a vast jackdaw-collection of examples and instances, tracing with their help the development of a sense of the past inherent in submerged, ignored or unofficial knowledge from the sixteenth century to the twentieth. This in itself is a valuable service. However, there is a problem in the author's use of terminology which is crucial. Samuel, for the purposes of his argument, chooses to treat 'history' and 'the past' as interchangeable terms, and few professional historians would accept this approach.

Samuel points to uses and manifestations of the past in, seemingly, everything possible; retrofittings around houses and architecture, *retrochic* in clothes, design, food, ornament and pop culture generally and, by far the most interesting and evocative part of his thesis, the emergence of new passions for the past as demonstrated by the post-1960s activities of 'resurrectionists' such as family historians, and by the rise of new forms of conservationism. In this latter connection he is able to demonstrate the sheer width of connotation of the term and concept Heritage.

> which has been broadened ... to take in not only the ivied church and village green, but also the terraced street, the railway cottages, the covered market and even the city slum; not only the water-meadows, such as those painted by Constable, but also the steam-powered machinery lovingly assembled in the industrial museums.[1]

Not only does the sheer scope and amorphousness of this idea, Heritage, seem to justify Robert Hewison's description of it as an 'industry',[2] its all-embracing character raises questions to do with the morality of word or expression, and one can be pretty certain that a George Orwell would have noticed the connection of Heritage with sheer opportunism in fashion, organization and business.

Samuel, then, has examined the popular appeal of the past and its endless permutations and manifestations of taste, activity and attraction, whether expressed through the theme park, the archaeological dig, the museum, the postcard sales point or the re-enacted battle; and, emerging dripping from the castle moat, he moves on to defend Heritage by suggesting that it has been the butt of intellectual and academic snobbery, the champions of which, like Hewison and Patrick Wright,[3] have gone on to erect a seeming conspiracy theory around it. Samuel should undoubtedly have considered the possibility that weightier historians may one day demonstrate more convincing connections between the Heritage upsurge and Britain's fortunes. There is a suggestive hypothesis here, to say the least, but our author is so beguiled by the sheer apparent vitality of the Heritage movement that he forgets that the latter has owed a great deal to the curious economy of Thatcherite Britain – which caused every other town to seek for tourists as a sometimes hopeless means of counteracting the destruction of industries and the realities of unemployment and insecurity. It has been a febrile vitality in all conscience.

The gifted and always intensely readable author has not found it difficult to place the ostensibly mass-educational and popular manifestations of Heritage alongside the earnest, sometimes narrow and fashion-dominated world of academic history, and to make judgements which from time to time reflect or coincide with some of those aired in the present study. But the argument in these pages does not claim that academic historians are an undifferentiated mass. Some are interested in the psychology and strategies of the educational process, others are not. Some can see a use for Heritage, others dislike its manifestations. Most are very critical of the idea of obtaining expertise in some branch of history without real and sustained effort, and many are rightly suspicious of the notion that exposure to Heritage can bring about such effort. Above all, Heritage concerns itself with *the Past*, however the latter is seen, and not with History as a coherent survey, process or analysis. It is Samuel's elision of Past into History which is dangerous. The one is not of course a synonym for the other: History is a skilled and informed way of interpreting the Past, which in any case has uncertain objective reality, but the implications of which have to be examined with care. Samuel regards academic historians as a tiresome and restrictive priesthood who prefer to ignore or discourage the mass of amateur and popular activity of which he writes.

Samuel's (1994) book will be read by mature students of local history in the years to come, and it may appeal to the prejudices of those students who enjoy collecting any manifestation of the past in their own localities. Samuel's historical colleagues, especially those who possess a sense of humour, will be intrigued by his blunderbuss or scatter-gun tactics, whereby he tries to demonstrate the immense variety of sources that have been supposedly neglected by historians: myths, songs, broadsheets, folk-tales, artefacts of all kinds, oral reminiscences, photographs. Although he tends to overwhelm the reader with the sheer prolixity of his examples, he also writes with a passion that one would associate with a relative newcomer (or convert) to the field. In fact he has been partly involved in it for many years, without having the continuous involvement of the present writer, and in his unmeasured enthusiasm Samuel has produced a very useful, if occasionally perverse, conspectus of the great field of non-academic antiquarianism. His enthusiasms bring a new freshness to some subjects, and in a well-documented chapter on 'The Discovery of Old Photographs' he has some decidedly interesting things to say, whilst at the same time forgetting that the Urban History Group was accepting the use of such sources back in the 1960s, and that the 'Current Bibliography of Urban History' listed collections of photographs from its inception in 1974. For all its headlong enthusiasm, or because of the latter, *Theatres of Memory* will sow confusion by very largely accepting the Heritage and conservationist movements at their own valuation – and here we should bear in mind that these forces in society have the full endorsement of a large part of the establishment as well as massive support from the media, national and local. Even the Labour Party, following the ideological lead of the Tory Party, has its Shadow Minister for National Heritage.

The thin red line against this massive movement consists of a relatively small body of professional historians, not all of whom are as restrictive, anti-popular and sunk in predictability as Samuel likes to suggest. Many are disturbed by the forces ranged against them; others take an optimistic line and trust that widespread obsession with the Past can lead to a suitable chemical conversion into History. To begin to perform this last, one would require an addition to the teaching strength of History amounting to several thousands of dynamic performers, who might then demonstrate that an interest in 'real' or 'serious' historical study does not mean that one turns one's back on cakes and ale, but instead that it expands and enriches the humanity of those who participate.

The qualification is that the cakes and ale are then enjoyed because they appear as the culmination of constructive and self-motivated effort. There is, in reality, little that is ultimately or permanently enriching in the mass of activity that Samuel describes. Much of it consists of situations leading to passive semi-involvement, as in the case of many visitors to museums, which are responsible for by far the largest sector presenting the past to the public. This sector appeals to the primitive antiquarian instincts (or pre-conditioning) of many millions of people

and, as is argued in the present volume (Chapter 3) it presents fragmented and ready-made impressions of the past, which in turn allow
little scope for independent judgement – for the customer or consumer
has learned to accept the idea of the semi-hidden expert who tells him
or her what to think. In the course of his or her fairly expensive family
journey round a museum that person will not only receive pre-packaged
history but a past occasionally processed into hyper-reality. It is true
that a minority of museum-users bring information and judgement to
what they see, but for them elaborate presentations are hardly called
for. The argument that deduces conspiracy theory in all of this is simply
misguided. The worthy members of the Museums Association who
think up ingenious displays are not a conspiracy, but just professional
people struggling to justify their existences without having the time to
see beyond their immediate concerns. They are in some respects more
specialized than the professional historians whom Samuel berates.

Such issues are by no means the most serious raised by Samuel's
general argument. Let us move from the subject of the largely passive
consumer of Heritage-owned sites and museums to that of the more
active pursuer of antiquarian concerns, who is involved in the collection
of individual facts and artefacts or the surveying and classifying of a
mass of *curiosa* from types of hay-waggon to designs of letter-box.
These activities can be extremely enjoyable, and mostly they harm
nobody. Some take the enthusiast into the open air with his or her
family, and where warnings or criticisms are made, it should be spelt
out that no critic is automatically a spoilsport. Most of the devotees of
these hobbies do not elevate their significance to some level of preten-
tiousness, and occasionally the enthusiast can be persuaded into a rather
wider form of involvement; the letter-boxes, after all, were a significant
part of postal history, and nearness or difficulty of communication has
great importance for human beings, just as design has significance for
the aesthetic aspirations of a society. However, the enthusiasm of the
antiquary is almost invariably centred on the discrete, the individual
object or site or building, or – even more importantly – the single
obsessive idea. Hence, single objects may derive their significance from
classes or classifications of similar items, but they are collected for their
individual value, to please the individual. In practice, few 'lone ranger'
antiquaries give the impression that they are handling their collected
artefacts as custodians for the public, and the rise of the metal-detector
enthusiast has been connected with a thriving trade in minor artefacts
such as Roman or other coins. In other words, the doubtless fashionable term 'commodification' has an all too genuine significance in such
cases, and an intense psychological individualism may easily become
economic in character and practice.

However, Samuel, in his chapter on 'Heritage-baiting', sweeps all such considerations aside, and instead brings in the question of snobbery directed against trade or business. This does indeed thrust us into a crucial debate as to whether well-publicized economic motives can always be disinterested, and the question is not necessarily rooted in snobbery, but rather in deeply founded suspicions further nourished by the rich manure of 'sleaze' in which the country's rulers seem to thrive. It is not wholly foolish to fear that a next general election but one or two might bring an England wherein every site, every artefact and every document has its price.

County and other learned societies are aware of an offensive undergrowth of trading and site-raiding activity, and so every effort is made to keep a protective eye on the established sites which are their main concern. Furthermore, the world of archaeology is tightly and indeed hierarchically organized, and its leading luminaries consciously operate on behalf of what they see as the public good. The anarchic market, towards which Samuel's argument seems to point, is in hard reality anathema to them – and it is fortunate that a form of authority reigns.

It is doubtless a compliment to Samuel's portrayal of this thriving world of interest in the past that his characterization raises a series of important and urgent questions. It is no accident that the major issue of fragmentation of historical study, discussed in the present volume (Chapter 2), has an exaggerated reflection in the world of autonomous and individualistic study and collection. We can easily envisage a situation wherein the isolated individual, in pursuing what interests him or her, has little or no concern with any wider framework or reference or criticism and the broader world which is thus inhabited consists of thousands of particles of disconnected activity, with uncertain standards, aims and justification – save that of the satisfaction of the ego. The word 'satisfaction' here raises another massive question, the Benthamite one of the greatest happiness of the greatest number, and that calls for careful discussion.

Meanwhile, we have already noted that academic and learned society archaeologists are tightly organized, and local historians, whilst achieving no such close organization, do in fact constantly tend to come together in national and local associations. Most towns and even villages now have their local history societies, and although the latter are often little more than arrangers of lectures and trips, their very existence raises questions of standards and aspiration. At the national level, bodies like the British Association for Local History have to confront such matters far more directly, and their main committees frequently contain academic representatives. The more general fragmentation of interest, topic and activity undoubtedly weakens the efforts of such bodies, yet the fact remains that dozens of local societies publish the results of their researches, and that national organizations (such as the Historical Association as well as the British Association for Local History) publish standard-setting guides and topic reviews in local history as best they can. A determinedly optimistic view (one which at the same time avoids fatuity) will be happy to place many local publications into the class of proto-history, whereby the authors have steeped themselves in some locally interesting field and at the same time derived satisfaction from the exercise. A minority of such works are undoubtedly of historical value, although, here again, the great majority of members of local history societies are passive consumers of lectures, and only one in ten may be a researcher. This is certainly the case in numerous examples known directly to the writer.

This is a very different picture from the seethingly active one portrayed by Samuel. The reality is a world made up largely of semi-passive consumers, persons and groups whose interest in a given topic extends for the length of a day out, people to whom little harm is done but who probably and equally gain little of lasting benefit to themselves. Those who are in some degree active, such as members of the mock battle squads in the Sealed Knot, gain excitement, exercise and friendship in activity which has little to do with a sustained study of other aspects of the past. At best they reap some special knowledge of a technical kind, and also something which could in other circumstances be very useful – a sense of the practicalities of seventeenth-century warfare, for example.

Indeed, it is possible to regard benignly much of this non-academic concern with the past, which seems harmless until one turns to examine some of its consequences for historical understanding and for the teaching of history in general. Let us simply adopt, first of all, the position that such understanding is not merely 'good' for the citizen, but is an indispensable part of his development, so much so as to be regarded as part of a citizen's birthright. Those historians and educationalists who have contributed to the History sections of the National Curriculum plainly have such considerations in mind but, these expert contributors do not wish their subject to be regarded as a form of nasty medicine. If it can be stimulative of willing learning, enjoyable argument and judgement, and, very often, fun and excitement, so much the better. But, teachers and taught are now (if we take Samuel's portrayal as seriously as it deserves) surrounded by a world of absorption, amusement, happy involvement and infectious fun – and, it might well appear, a world in which academic standards of care, discipline and judgement are to be circumvented, and a world in which valuable results can be obtained with limited effort, or no effort at all. In such circumstances the territory of organized school or other study will appear to be unappealing and unappetizing, and the snippets of disconnectedly erudite information produced by the elders of the local history society may merely add to the confusion and to the undermining of historical approaches, however straightforward.

Samuel apparently senses that his argument is weak or dubious at this point, and he asserts (a little defensively, perhaps?) that 'there is no reason to think that people are more passive when looking at old photographs of film footage, handling a museum exhibit, following a local history trail, or even buying an historical souvenir, than when reading a book'.[4] The author justifies this claim by the statement that 'as in any reading, they assimilate (images) as best they can to pre-existing images and narratives. The pleasures of the gaze ... are different in kind from those of the written word but not necessarily less taxing on historical reflection and thought.'[5] The necessary rejoinder here is that everything depends on the framework and circumstances in which the gazing, handling or reading is taking place. Let us assume immediately that a passionate collector or treasure-hunter will concentrate immediately on the object that is intriguing, but for only so long as to enable that person to reach a restricted goal. But a person with a measure of historical training, however elementary, will most certainly refer back to 'pre-existing images and narratives' and will then actively absorb his or her images of the items examined into a growing body of knowledge and experience. The person will not do this immediately, because observation is a highly complex process, and he or she will be puzzled by many things that are seen and, accordingly, that person may need help from a more experienced individual.

But in a situation wherein motivation and stimulus are largely absent, the gaze is all too likely to be one of vacancy. There is much to be learned about the effects of museum displays, photographs, documents, films and historical scenes on children and adults in differing situations, and the accumulation of real knowledge has been hindered by the tendency of history teachers to write articles claiming success in the use of visual and other aids, when in fact the most rigorously controlled experiments have been called for. Given these caveats, there is little doubt that museum and Heritage displays can be used effectively if discriminatingly by skilled history teachers, who at the same time enjoy the advantages of academic training. About one thing we can be absolutely certain: only the most gifted youngster or adult will teach him or herself a great deal that is systematic, discriminating and comprehensible from the vast and varied flood of information that comes under the guise of Heritage. Yet, to leave the citizen, young or old, without any critical faculty is to turn him or her on to the open sea without a means of propulsion or navigation.

There still remains the argument that to leave people to innocent antiquarian pursuits is to increase the stock of felicity within society at any one time, representing the supposed greatest happiness of the greatest number. This consideration weighs heavily with many informed and humane academic historians, who realize that only a minority of people will ever aspire to develop the skilled and specialized view of the professional historian, and who have come to recognize, albeit resignedly, that the snares of antiquarianism will entrap many of those who remain fascinated by the past. Let them therefore (the argument goes) seek as much happiness and incidental self-fulfilment as they can find in archaeological site, church interior, stately home and convenient record office. As has been pointed out in the present book,[6] this means that one's fellow-citizens are then relegated into a lower and second-class order or caste, and to hold such a view, in a democratic society, cannot be inspiring for the person who adopts it.

We shall at the same time recognize reality by accepting that thousands of people *do* find happiness in simple compilation and, of course, thousands of family historians are in this position. This book has suggested (for example in Chapter 7) ways by which this large group can be brought into a wider discourse, one which can only be of benefit to themselves and which should certainly not deprive them of such happiness as they have enjoyed. It will be appropriate at this point to mention that Bentham was distinguished for other ideas besides that of his famous calculus of pain and pleasure, and that he was also deeply interested in education, and was in that respect an admirer of Robert Owen's scheme for the education of factory children at New Lanark. In other words, he believed in the improvement of the individual before the latter was thrown into the world to become the autonomous judge of his best interests. There is a moral here, to the extent that academics, and historians, cannot wash their hands of responsibility for fellow-citizens.

And what are the mechanics of the world in which the latter may experience happiness? This world is turning out to be one in which leisure time for many people is diminishing, notwithstanding the promise of a working week heavily reduced by technology. Lack of leisure means lack of freedom. Unrestricted working hours, operative in far too many small firms or businesses, can of course be limited under the pressure of public opinion, but there is little doubt that job insecurity, fear and pressure in work itself are alike widespread at this time.

Let us say that a victim of conditions like these could well find consolation in some kind of study of the past, which at the same time takes him or her away from the sources of worry or strain. Here, however, we encounter two telling considerations: first, antiquarian or archaeological pursuits can be notoriously time-consuming, involving travel, note-taking, drawing, photography, correspondence and discussion. Secondly, county and city record offices (which spend much of their time supplying enquirers with what is ultimately antiquarian information) are closed at weekends, and will be open only to the man or woman who does not work fixed shop or office hours, but who may be able to take advantage of shift working to call in before five in the afternoon. In such circumstances, time becomes markedly precious, and it is at this point that the academic, who does have some allocated time to devote to historical study, begins to feel horror at what looks like wasted endeavour on the part of many fellow-citizens – who are plainly not learning anything about the wider society of which they are members, and are learning very little about past societies. Without a sense of social change and at least an awareness of the basic mechanics of history, the citizen is hindered from understanding both rights and responsibilities.

Meanwhile, the varied and complex administrative apparatus of record offices, museums and libraries – which between them supply the raw material of documentation, books and general information, without which investigation into the past cannot proceed – were in general founded for the education of the public. The rise of this information-giving apparatus has seemed to be almost fortuitous over the last century, and it is unfortunately dependent on public provision and investment which is now likely to be curtailed unless it fulfils break-even criteria. The vast output of information for which these institutions are responsible has itself created the idea that they can be used for forms of leisure activity – now partially amusement or pastime, in the sense that such activities do not, and sometimes cannot, operate within an established educational framework. This apart, there has been an enormous rise of interest in the past, as Samuel's own writings show, and it may be that this is not so much evidence of 'decline' as of the growth of rootlessness and insecurity. It is this last malady which may well go far towards explaining the hold of antiquarianism on so many people; after all, it is considerable solace to be able to contemplate a past which appears to carry unchanging certainties and values – those of deeply founded tradition, the solidifications of building style, procedures hallowed by use and custom, the certainties of the past which appear to reside in an archaeological site. Family historians, too, engage in a search for roots and 'ancient-ness' as demonstrated by the constant recurrence of a family name, and there can be little doubt that their initial impulses are antiquarian in this sense. But a genealogical table is also a record of people, not inert objects, and the investigator with imagination can quickly learn the distinction.

As for Heritage itself, there is only one thing to say: there is surely something wrong with a society that can devote so much investment to displays of the-past-as-diversion, and can yet regard with apparent toleration just as many points of educational deprivation in our schools.

To conclude: it should be noted that Raphael Samuel writes not as a defender of establishments, but as a socialist who is determined to jolt both historians and fellow socialists into an appreciation of the apparent ramifications of popular taste and interest past and present. It would be a foolish individual who turned his or her back on such knowledge, or who refused to use it for educational purposes. It may be that much history teaching in the future will use a far greater variety of material and illustrations than ever before; but is it likely to be given such resources, in the light of trends in the financing of British state education? It appears much more likely that the business side of 'history' has emerged triumphant – and perhaps a conventional or Old Labour socialist view may be gloomily justified after all, or may at least have an unquenchable optimism duly tempered.

Notes

1. Samuel, R. (1994), *Theatres of Memory, Vol. 1: Past and Present in Contemporary Culture*, Verso: London, 151. The sections dealing with Heritage are mainly at pp. 205–312.
2. Hewison (1987), *The Heritage Industry: Britain in a Climate of Decline*, Methuen: London, *passim*.
3. Hewison (1987), *passim*; Wright, P. (1985), *On Living in an Old Country: The National Past in Contemporary Britain*, Verso: London. This last is a subtly argued text which perhaps lacks the impact and approach to solidify the notion of 'decline' in this kind of debate.
4. Samuel (1994), 271.
5. Ibid.
6. *Vide* Chapter 3, 59.

Bibliography

Addy, J. (1989), *Sin and Society in the Seventeenth Century*, Routledge: London.

Agnew, J.A. (1987), *Place and Politics: The Geographical Mediation of State and Society*, Allen and Unwin: Boston.

Armitt, M.L. (ed. Willingham F. Rawnsley), (1916), *Rydal*, Titus Wilson: Kendal.

Ashton, T.S. (1958), inaugural statement, *Business History*, (1), December.

Barwell, J. (1990), 'Museums and the National Curriculum', *Teaching History*, October.

Bell, C. and Newby, H. (1971), *Community Studies: An Introduction to the Sociology of the Local Community*, Allen and Unwin: London.

Beresford, M.W. (1954), *The Lost Villages of England*, Lutterworth Press: London.

Blackwood, B.G. (1978), *The Lancashire Gentry and the Great Rebellion, 1640–1660*, Chetham Soc., **25**, Manchester.

Briggs, A. (1958), review, 'The Leicester School', *New Statesman and Nation*, 15 February.

———— (1963), *Victorian Cities*, Odhams: London.

Brooks, F.W. (1973), 'Local History, 1930–48', *Local Historian*, **10**, (8).

Burnett, A.D. and Taylor, P.J. (eds) (1981), *Political Studies from Spatial Perspectives: Anglo-American Essays on Political Geography*, Wiley: Chichester, New York, Brisbane, Toronto.

Butlin, R.A. (1990), 'Regions in England and Wales, *c*. 1600–1914' in R.A. Dodgshon and R.A. Butlin *An Historical Geography of England and Wales*, 2nd edn, Academic Press: London.

Cannadine, D. (1980), *Lords and Landlords: The Aristocracy and the Towns, 1774–1967*, Leicester University Press: Leicester.

Celoria, F. (1958), *Teach Yourself Local History*, English Universities Press: London.

Chambers, J.D. (1932), *Nottinghamshire in the Eighteenth Century*, P.S. King: London.

———— (1953), 'Enclosure and Labour Supply in the Industrial Revolution', *Economic History Review*, 5, reprinted (1965) in D.V. Glass, and D.E.C. Eversley, *Population in History: Essays in Historical Demography*, Arnold: London.

———— (1957), *The Vale of Trent*, reprinted as *Economic History Review*, Supplement No. 3, Cambridge University Press: Cambridge.

Chisholm, M. (1975), *Human Geography: Evolution or Revolution?*, Pelican: Harmondsworth.

Clapham, J.H. (1950), *An Economic History of Modern Britain* (reprint of 2nd edition, original dated 1926), vol. 1, Cambridge University Press: Cambridge.

Clark, P. and Souden, D. (1988), *Migration in Early Modern England*, Hutchinson: London.

Court, W.H.B. (1938), *The Rise of the Midland Industries, 1600–1838*, Oxford University Press: Oxford.

Cox, D. (1965), 'Antiquarianism and Local History', *Local Historian*, 6, (8).

Crafts, N.F.R. (1978), 'Enclosure and Labour Supply Revisited', *Explorations in Economic History*, 15.

Cowper, H.S. (1899), *Hawkshead: Its History, Architecture, Industries, Folklore and Dialect*, Bemrose: London and Derby.

Daniels, G.W. (1920), *The Early English Cotton Industry, with some Unpublished Letters of Samuel Crompton*, Manchester University Press: Manchester.

Davies, M.F. (1909), *Life in An English Village: An Economic and Historical Survey of the Parish of Corsley in Wiltshire*, T. Fisher Unwin: London.

Dickinson, R.E. (1964), *City and Region*, Routledge: London.

Dodd, A.H. (1933), *The Industrial Revolution in North Wales*, University of Wales Press Board: Cardiff.

Dodgshon, R.A. and Butlin, R.A. (1990), 'Regions in England and Wales', in *An Historical Geography of England and Wales*, 2nd edn, Academic Press: London.

Drake, M. (ed.) (1994), *Time, Family, Community: A Perspective on Family and Community History*, Open University: Milton Keynes.

Duncan, S.S. and Savage, M. (1989), 'Space, Scale and Locality', *Antipode*, 21, (3).

Dymond, D.P. (1974), *Archaeology and History: A Plea for Reconciliation*, Thames and Hudson: London.

Dyos, H.J. (1955), 'Railways and Housing in Victorian London', *Journal of Transport History*, 2, (1) and (2), May and November.

———— (1957), 'Counting the Cost of Railways', *Amateur Historian*, 4, (1).

———— (1961), *Victorian Suburb: A Study of the Growth of Camberwell*, Leicester University Press: Leicester.

Dyos, H.J. and Wolff, M. (eds) (1973), *The Victorian City: Images and Realities*, 2 vols, Routledge: London.

Eco, U. (1987), *Travels in Hyper-Reality*, Picador: London.

Elton, G.R. (1969), *The Practice of History*, Fontana: London.

Emmison, F.G. (1978), *Introduction to Archives*, Phillimore: Chichester.

Everitt, A.M. (1961), 'The Study of Local History', *Amateur Historian*, 6, (2).

——— (1966), *The Community of Kent and the Great Rebellion*, Leicester University Press: Leicester.

——— (1969), *The Local Community and the Great Rebellion*, Historical Association: London.

Everitt, A.M. and Tranter, M, (1978), *Local History at Leicester, 1948–78: A Bibliography of Writings by Members of the Department of English Local History*, University of Leicester: Leicester.

Eversley, D.E.C. (1956), 'A Survey of Population in an Area of Worcestershire from 1660 to 1850, on the Basis of Parish Records', *Population Studies*, 10.

Eversley, D.E.C., Laslett, P. and Wrigley, E.A. (eds) (1966), *An Introduction to English Historical Demography*, Weidenfeld and Nicolson: London.

Fieldhouse, R. and Jennings, B. (1978), *A History of Richmond and Swaledale*, Phillimore: Chichester.

Fieldhouse, R. (1985a), *Adult Education and the Cold War: Academic Values under Siege, 1946–51*, Department of Adult Education, University of Leeds: Leeds.

——— (1985b), 'Conformity and Confrontation in English Responsible Body Adult Education, 1925–50', *Studies in the Education of Adults*, 17, (2).

Finberg, H.P.R. (1952), *The Local Historian and his Theme*, Leicester University Press: Leicester.

——— (1955), *Gloucestershire: The Making of the English Landscape*, Hodder: London.

——— (1962), 'Local History', in H.P.R. Finberg (ed.), *Approaches to History*, Routledge: London.

——— (1967), 'The Local Historian and his Theme', in H.P.R. Finberg and V.H.T. Skipp, *Local History, Objective and Pursuit*, David and Charles: Newton Abbot.

Fitzhugh, T. (1952), Editorial in *Amateur Historian*, 1, (1), August–September.

Foster, J, and Sheppard, J. (1982), *British Archives: A Guide to Archives in the United Kingdom*, Macmillan: London.

Frankenberg, R. (1966), *Communities in Britain: Social Life in Town and Country*, Penguin: Harmondsworth.

Garside, P. (1978), 'Local History in Undergraduate History Courses', *Local Historian*, 13, (2).

Giddens, A. (1981), *A Contemporary Critique of Historical Materialism: Vol. 1, Power, Property and the State*, Macmillan: London.

Grace, F. (1992), *The Late Victorian Town*, British Association for Local History: London.

Grigg, D. (1967), 'Regions, Models and Classes', in R.J. Chorley and P. Haggett, (eds), *Integrated Models in Geography*, Methuen: London.

Harrison, J.F.C. (1961), *Learning and Living, 1790–1960: A Study in the History of the Adult Education Movement*, Routledge: London.

Harte, N.B. (1977), 'Trends in Publication on the Economic and Social History of Great Britain and Ireland, 1925–74', *Economic History Review* 30, (1).

Harvie, C. (1994), *The Rise of Regional Europe*, Routledge: London.

Hawley, A. (1950), *Human Ecology: A Theory of Community Structure*, Ronald Press: New York.

Heaton, H. (1920), *The Yorkshire Woollen and Worsted Industry*, Oxford Historical and Literary Studies 10, Clarendon Press: Oxford.

Hewison, R. (1987), *The Heritage Industry; Britain in a Climate of Decline*, Methuen: London.

Hey, D.G. (1974), *An English Rural Community: Myddle under the Tudors and Stuarts*, Leicester University Press: Leicester.

——— (1986), *Family History and Local History in England*, Longman: London.

Hillery, G.J. Jr (1968), *Communal Organizations: A Study of Local Societies*, University of Chicago Press: Chicago and London.

Hindle, B.P. (1988), *Maps for Local History*, Batsford: London.

Hobsbawm, E.J. (1980), 'The Revival of Narrative: Some Comments', *Past and Present*, 86.

——— (1995), *The Age of Extremes: The Short Twentieth Century 1914–1991*, Michael Joseph: London.

Holmes, C., (1980), *Seventeenth Century Lincolnshire*, History of Lincolnshire Series, 7, History of Lincolnshire Committee: Lincoln.

Horn, P. (1976), *Labouring Life in the Victorian Countryside*, Gill and Macmillan: Dublin and London.

Hoskins, W.G. (1935), *Industry, Trade and People in Exeter, 1688–1800*, first edition, Manchester University Press: Manchester.

——— (1937), 'The Fields of Wigston Magna', *Transactions of the Leicester Archaeological Society*, 19.

——— (1952), 'The Writing of Local History', *History Today*, 2, (1).

——— (1955), *The Making of the English Landscape*, Hodder: London.

——— (1956), 'Fieldwork in Local History', *Amateur Historian*, 3, (1), Autumn.

——— (1957a), 'The Population of an English Village, 1066–1801', in *Transactions of the Leicestershire Archaeological Society*, 33.

———— (1957b), *The Midland Peasant: the Economic and Social History of a Leicestershire Village*, Macmillan: London.

———— (1959), *Local History in England*, Longman: London.

———— (1965), *Provincial England: Essays in Social and Economic History*, Macmillan: London and New York.

———— (1966), *English Local History: The Past and the Future* (inaugural lecture), Leicester University Press: Leicester.

———— (1967), *Fieldwork in Local History*, Faber: London.

Howell, C. (1983), *Land, Family and Inheritance in Transition: Kibworth Harcourt, 1280–1700*, Leicester University Press: Leicester.

Howkins, A. (1986), 'The Discovery of Rural England', in R. Colls and P. Dodd (eds), *Englishness, Politics and Culture, 1880–1920*, Croom Helm: London and Brighton.

Hudson, P. (ed.) (1989), *Regions and Industries: A Perspective on the Industrial Revolution in Britain*, Cambridge University Press: Cambridge.

———— (1992), 'Land, the Social Structure and Industry in Two Yorkshire Townships, 1660–1800', in P. Swan and D. Foster (eds), *Essays in Regional and Local History*, Hutton Press: Beverley.

Hughes, A. (1982), 'Warwickshire on the Eve of the Civil War: A County Community?', *Midland History*, 7.

———— (1987), *Politics, Society and Civil War in Warwickshire, 1620–1660*, Cambridge University Press: Cambridge.

Iredale, D. (1973), *Enjoying Archives: What They Are, Where to Find Them and How to Use Them*, David and Charles: Newton Abbot.

James, T. (1987), 'Using Local History in the GCSE: A Practical Exercise on the Leawood Canal', *Local History*, (15).

Jennings, B. (1970) (ed.), *A History of Harrogate and Knaresborough*, Advertiser Press: Knaresborough. (See also Fieldhouse.)

———— (1992), 'Authors by the Score: Adult Education Classes and the Writing of Local History', *Local Historian*, 22, (2).

Jones, P.M. (1981), 'Parish, Seigneurie and the Community of Inhabitants in Southern Central France During the Eighteenth and Nineteenth Centuries', *Past and Present*, 91.

Kaye, H.J. (1984), *The British Marxist Historians*, Cambridge University Press: Cambridge.

Kellett, J.R. (1969), *The Impact of Railways on Victorian Cities*, Routledge: London.

Knowles, C.H. (*c.* 1983), *Landscape History*, Historical Association: London.

König, R. (1968), (trans. E. Fitzgerald), *The Community*, Routledge: London.

Lambert, T.A. (1972), 'Generations and Change: Towards a Theory of Generations as a Force in Historical Process', *Youth and Society*, 4.

Laslett, P. (1965), *The World We Have Lost*, Methuen: London.

Lawler, U.R.E. (1978), *North-Western Theses and Dissertations, 1950–1978*, Occasional Paper, Centre for NW Regional Studies, University of Lancaster: Lancaster. (Supplement to foregoing, 1979–88, Centre for NW Regional Studies.)

Lee, C.H. (1971), *Regional Economic Growth in the United Kingdom since the 1880s*, McGraw-Hill: Maidenhead.

——— (1980), 'Regional Structural Change in the Long Run: Britain, 1841–1971', in S. Pollard (ed.), *Region und Industrialisierung: Studien zur Rolle der Region in der Wirtschaftsgeschichte der letzten zwei Jahrhunderts*, Vandenhoeck and Ruprecht: Göttingen.

——— (1986), *The British Economy since 1700*, Cambridge University Press: Cambridge.

Lee, J.M. (1963), *Social Leaders and Public Persons*, Manchester University Press: Manchester.

Levine, P. (1986), *The Amateur and the Professional: Antiquarians, Historians and Archaeologists in Victorian England, 1838–1866*, Cambridge University Press: Cambridge.

Levine, D. and Wrightson, K. (1979), *Poverty and Piety in an English Village: Terling, 1525–1700*, Academic Press: London.

Lewis, C. (1989), *Particular Places: An Introduction to English Local History*, London Library: London.

Lewis, G.J. (1979), *Rural Communities*, David and Charles: Newton Abbot.

Lord, E. (1991), 'The Boundaries of Local History: A discussion paper', *Journal of Regional and Local Studies*, 2, (1–2).

Lowenthal, D. and Binney, M. (1981) *Our Past Before Us: Why Do We Save It?*, Temple Smith: London.

Macfarlane, A. with Harrison, S. and Jardine C. (1977a), *Reconstructing Historical Communities*, Cambridge University Press: Cambridge.

Macfarlane, A. (1977b), 'The Study of Communities', *Social History*, 5, May.

Machin, R. (1977), 'The Great Rebuilding: an assessment', *Past and Present*, 77.

Mannheim, K. (1952), 'The Problem of Generations', in P. Kecskemeti (ed.), *Essays on the Sociology of Knowledge*, Routledge: London.

Marshall, J.D. (1963), 'The Use of Local History: Some Comments', *Amateur Historian*, 6, (1).

——— (1965), 'The Use of Local History', *Local Historian*, 6, (7).

——— (1983), 'The Rise and Transformation of the Cumbrian Market Town 1660–1900', *Northern History*, 19.

———— (1984), 'Cumberland and Westmorland Societies in London, 1734–1914', *Transactions of the Cumberland and Westmorland Antiquarian and Archaeological Society* (NS), 84.

———— (ed.) (1990), 'Are British Regions Neglected?', symposium in *Journal of Regional and Local Studies*, 10, (2).

———— (1992), 'Proving Ground or the Creation of Regional Identity? The Origins and Problems of Regional History in Britain', in P. Swan and D. Foster (eds), *Essays in Regional and Local History*, Hutton Press: Beverley.

———— (1995), 'Out of Wedlock: Perceptions of a Cumbrian Social Problem in the Victorian Context', *Northern History*, 30, 194–207.

Marshall, J.D. and Walton, J.K. (1981), *The Lake Counties from 1830 to the mid-Twentieth Century*, Manchester University Press: Manchester.

McIntosh, M.K. (1986), *Autonomy and Community: The Royal Manor of Havering, 1200–1500*, Cambridge University Press: Cambridge.

———— (1991), *A Community Transformed: The Manor and Liberty Havering, 1500–1620*, Cambridge University Press: Cambridge.

Mills, D.R. (1993), Local Population Studies Society *Newsletter*, (10), January.

———— (1994), 'Community and Nation in the Past: Perceptions and Reality', in M. Drake (ed.), *Time, Family, Community: A Perspective on Family and Community History*, Open University: Milton Keynes.

Millward, Roy (1955), *Lancashire: The Making of the English Landscape*, Hodder: London.

Mitson, A. (1993), 'The Significance of Kinship Networks in the Seventeenth Century: South-West Nottinghamshire', in C. Phythian-Adams (ed.), *Societies, Culture and Kinship 1580–1850: Cultural Provinces and English Local History*, Leicester University Press: Leicester.

Moon, M. (1851) *A History, Topography and Directory of Westmorland etc.*, (reprint, Whitehaven, 1978) Mannex: Beverley.

Munby, L.M. (1977), 'Reminiscences and Reflections of an Ex-Editor', *Local Historian*, 12, (7).

———— (1992), 'Reflections on Times Past', *Local Historian*, 22, (1).

Noble, M. and Crowther, J. (1992), 'Adult Education and the Development of Regional and Local History: East Yorkshire and North Lincolnshire, c.1929–1985', in P. Swan and D. Foster (eds), *Essays in Regional and Local History*, Hutton Press: Beverley.

Oliver, G.A. (1989), *Photographs and Local History*, Batsford: London.

Olney, R.J. (1979), *Rural Society and Country Government in Nineteenth Century Lincolnshire*, History of Lincolnshire Series, 10, Lincoln.

Orwell, G. (1962a), Essay on 'Boys' Weeklies', *Inside the Whale and Other Essays*, Penguin: Harmondsworth.

———— (1962b), Essay on 'Politics and the English language', *Inside the Whale and Other Essays*, Penguin: Harmondsworth.

Paasi, A. (1991), 'Deconstructing Regions: Notes on the Scale of Spatial Life' *Environment and Planning*, 23, (2).

Parker, C. (1990), *The English Historical Tradition*, John Donald: Edinburgh.

Pelling, H. (1967), *The Social Geography of British Elections, 1885–1910*, Macmillan: London and New York.

Perkin, H. (1976), *The Age of the Automobile*, Quartet Books: London.

Phythian-Adams, C. (1987, revised 1991), *Rethinking Local History*, Department of English Local History Occasional Paper, No. 1, Leicester University Press: Leicester.

———— 'Hoskins's England: A Local Historian of Genius and the Realization of his Theme', *Local Historian*, 22, (4), November.

———— (1993a) (ed.), *Societies, Cultures and Kinship, 1580–1850: Cultural Provinces and English Local History*, Leicester University Press: Leicester.

———— (1993b), 'Local History and Societal History', *Local Population Studies*, 51.

Plant, Raymond (1974), *Community and Ideology: An Essay on Applied Social Philosophy*, Routledge: London.

Pollard, S. (1959), *A History of Labour in Sheffield*, Liverpool University Press: Liverpool.

Pollard, S. and Marshall, J.D. (1953), 'The Furness Railway and the Growth of Barrow', *Journal of Transport History*, 1, (1).

Porter, S. (1990), *Exploring Urban History: Sources for Local Historians*, Batsford: London.

Powell, W.R. (1958), 'Local history in theory and practice', *Bulletin of the Institute of Historical Research*, 31.

Pugh, R.B. (1954), *How to Write a Parish History*, 6th edn, Allen and Unwin: London.

Rea, T. (1988), 'A Local Study at Tutbury Hill', *Local History*, (16), January.

Read, D. (1964), 'The Use of Local History: The Local History of Modern Times', *Amateur Historian*, 6, (4).

Report of the Committee to Review Local History (Blake Committee) (1979), issued by Miss B. Miller, 26 Bedford Square, London WC1B 3HU.

Riden, P. (1987), *Record Sources for Local History*, Batsford: London.

Rix, M. (1953), 'Industrial Archaeology', *Amateur Historian*, 11, (8).

Roberts, E. (1984), *A Woman's Place: An Oral History of Working-Class Women between 1890 and 1940*, Blackwell: Oxford.

———— (1995), *Women and Families: An Oral History*, Blackwell: Oxford.

Robinson, W.S. (1950), 'Ecological Correlation and the Behaviour of Individuals', *American Sociological Review*, **15**.

Rogers, A. (ed.) (1977), *Group Projects in Local History*, Dawson, for the National Institute of Adult Education: London.

———— (1980) Review in *Local Historian*, **14**, (4).

———— (1995), 'Participatory Research in Local History', *Journal of Regional and Local Studies*, **15**, (1).

Rollison, D. (1981), 'Property, Ideology and Popular Culture in a Gloucestershire Village, 1660–1740', *Past and Present*, **93**.

———— (1992), *The Local Origins of Modern Society: Gloucestershire, 1500–1800*, Routledge: London.

Rowse, A.L. (1941), *Tudor Cornwall: Portrait of a Society*, Cape: London.

Samuel, R. (1976), 'Local History and Oral History', *History Workshop Journal*, (1), Spring.

———— (1979), 'Urban History and Local History', *History Workshop Journal*, (8), Autumn.

———— (ed.) (1981), *People's History and Socialist Theory*, Routledge: London.

———— (1994), *Theatres of Memory, Vol. 1: Past and Present in Contemporary Culture*, Verso: London.

Savage, M. (1987), *The Dynamics of Working-Class Politics: The Labour Movement in Preston, 1980–1940*, Cambridge University Press: Cambridge.

———— (1990a), 'The Rise of the Labour Party in Local Perspective', *Journal of Regional and Local Studies*, **10**, (1).

———— (1990b), 'People's History and the Local', *Journal of Regional and Local Studies*, **10**, (1), Summer.

Saxelby, C.H. (ed.), (1953), *Bolton Survey*, Bolton Geographical and Historical Associations: Bolton.

Sharpe, P. (1991), 'Literally Spinsters; a New Interpretation of Local Economy and Demography in Colyton in the Seventeenth and Eighteenth Centuries', *Economic History Review*, **44**, (1).

Skipp, V.H.T. (1981), 'Local History, a New Definition, Part 1', *Local Historian*, **14**, (6).

———— (1981), 'Local History, a New Definition and its Implications, Part 2', *Local Historian*, **14**, (7).

Snell, K.M.D. (1985), *Annals of the Labouring Poor: Social Change and Agrarian England, 1660–1900*, Cambridge University Press: Cambridge.

Spufford, M. (1973), 'The Total History of Village Communities', *Local Historian*, 10, (8).

————— (1974), *Contrasting Communities: English Villagers in the Sixteenth and Seventeenth Centuries*, Cambridge University Press: Cambridge.

————— (1974), 'Population Mobility in Pre-Industrial England', *Genealogists' Magazine*, 17, (9), March, 475.

————— (1974), 'Population Mobility in Pre-Industrial England', *Genealogists' Magazine*, 17, (10), June, 537.

Spufford, P. (1973), 'Population Mobility in Pre-Industrial England', *Genealogists' Magazine*, 17, (8), December, 420.

Stacey, M. (1960), *Tradition and Change: A Study of Banbury*, Cambridge University Press: Cambridge.

————— (1969), 'The Myth of Community Studies', *British Journal of Sociology*, 20.

Stephens, W.B. (1973), *Sources for English Local History*, Manchester University Press: Manchester.

Stuart, D. (1975), *County Borough: the History of Burton-on-Trent, 1901–74: Part I, Edwardian Burton*, Charter Trustees: Burton-on-Trent.

————— (1992), *Manorial Records: An Introduction to their Transcription and Translation*, Phillimore: Chichester.

Sutcliffe, Anthony (1975), 'The Condition of Urban History in England', *Local Historian*, 11, (5).

Tate, W.E. (1946), *The Parish Chest*, Cambridge University Press: Cambridge.

Thirsk, J. (1963), 'Work in Progress', *Agricultural History Review*, 11, (1).

Thomas, E. (1985), in M. Justin Davis (ed.), *A Literary Pilgrim; an Illustrated Guide to Britain's Literary Heritage*, Exeter.

Thomas, K. (1971), *Religion and the Decline of Magic*, Cambridge University Press: Cambridge.

Thompson, F.M.L. (1974), *Hampstead, Building a Borough, 1650–1964*, Routledge: London.

Thoyts, E.E. (1980), *How to Decipher and Study Old Documents*, 2nd edn, Elliot Stock: London.

Tiller, K. (1992), *English Local History: An Introduction*. Alan Sutton: Stroud.

Tönnies, F. (1955), *Community and Society* (trans. C.P. Loomis), Routledge: London and New York.

Trescatheric, B. (1981), 'The Furness Colony: The History of an Emigration Society in Great Britain and Minnesota from 1872 to c.1882', M. Litt., University of Lancaster.

Tupling, G.H. (1927), *The Economic History of Rossendale*, Economic History Series, Manchester University Press: Manchester.

Urdank, A.M. (1990), *Religion and Society in a Cotswold Vale: Nailsworth, Gloucestershire, 1780–1865*, University of California Press: Berkeley and Los Angeles.

Wadsworth, A.P. and Mann, J. de L. (1931), *The Cotton Trade and Industrial Lancashire, 1600–1780*, Manchester University Press: Manchester.

Walsh, W.H. (1962), 'History and Theory', *Encounter*, 18, (6).

West, J. (1962, 1982), *Village Records*, Macmillan: London.

———— (1983), *Town Records*, Phillimore: Chichester.

Williams, R. (1961), *The Long Revolution*, Chatto and Windus: London.

———— (1973), *The Country and the City*, Chatto and Windus: London.

———— (1977), *Marxism and Literature*, Oxford University Press: Oxford.

Williams, W.M. (1963), *A West Country Village: Ashworthy*, Routledge: London.

Winter, G. (1975), *The Golden Years, 1903–13*, David and Charles: Newton Abbot.

Wright, P. (1985), *On Living in an Old Country: The National Past in Contemporary Britain*, Verso: London.

Wrightson, K. and Levine, D. (1991), *The Making of an Industrial Society: Whickham, 1560–1765*, Oxford University Press: Oxford.

Wrigley, E.A. (1964, 1965), 'Parish registers and population history', *Amateur Historian*, 6, (5) and (6).

———— (1966), 'Family Limitation in Pre-industrial England', *Economic History Review*, 19, (1), April.

———— (1975), 'Baptism Coverage in Early Nineteenth Century England: The Colyton Area', *Population Studies*, 29.

———— (1977), 'The Changing Occupational Structure of Colyton over Two Centuries', *Local Population Studies*, 18.

Wrigley, E.A. and Schofield, R. (1981), *Population History of England, 1541–1871; a Reconstruction*, Edward Arnold: London.

Index

These entries refer largely to items and individuals in the book text. A few references are to additional data in the notes.